MORE GEMS OF GRACE

By the same author

MORE GEMS OF GRACE

Bob Stokes

LAKELAND
116 BAKER STREET
LONDON W1M 2BB

Copyright © Bob Stokes 1975

First Published 1975

ISBN 0 551 00554 8

Typesetting by Trade Linotype Ltd., Birmingham

Printed in Great Britain by
J. W. Arrowsmith Ltd., Bristol

Commendation

A theologian of great repute has said that, "There is no greater argument for the reality of authentic Christianity than a life transformed by the grace of God."

This is what makes the original *Gems of Grace*, and now its companion *More Gems of Grace*, both significant and satisfying in today's enquiring world. It is significant because it illustrates the power of God's transforming grace: it is satisfying because it relates to human situations as we really know them.

I warmly recommend this little book.

STEPHEN F. OLFORD

Dedication

Dedicated to my children and grandchildren—Peter, his wife Aileen with their family, Karen, Alison, Heather and Bradley; Gillian, her husband Warren with their family Darren and Timothy, all in Melbourne, Australia; Ruth, serving TWR as my personal efficient Secretary; and Jennifer with her husband Trevor in Jamaica.

Contents

Acknowledgment

The author is greatly indebted to those who helped in the publication of this book, especially to his devoted wife Cynthia and efficient daughter Ruth who painstakingly checked the proofs, and to Mrs Irene Phillips who cheerfully typed out many of the manuscripts in spite of physical weakness and ailing health.

1 Grannie's Greenhouse

*Whatsoever ye do, do it heartily as to
the Lord.*   Col. 3: 23)

It was a glorious summer day and my brother Alan,
and I, were staying with our Grannie in her delightful
old Georgian home in Epping, Essex. We always loved
this quaint old place, with its fascinating staircase
winding its way up three flights; the steep descent into
the cool spacious cellar; the cobble-stoned courtyard;
the sweet-scented syringa bushes forming a delightful
shrubbery through which you had to pass before entering the spacious garden with its miniature box hedges
and scented rose trees. Yes, all these leave the most
fragrant memories of our boyhood days.

Grannie Wright was cared for by two of her devoted
daughters, one of whom ran a small but efficient
private school. We always loved to spend a few weeks
of our holidays with them. It conjured up home-grown
strawberries, tennis parties, the weekly open market
with cheap-jacks offering all kinds of wonderful
bargains, and delightful walks and pony rides in Epping
Forest. Recently I drove past this old place, now converted into a tailoring establishment. Nothing remains
of the past but memories, and the garden is a
wilderness—my Grannie and her daughters have long
since passed away.

To get back to our story, Alan and I were at a loose
end one day, when we spotted some delightful plums
dangling most temptingly from a branch of a tree next
door. These could only be obtained by scaling the wall
underneath, and it so happened that adjacent to this

wall was my Grannie's greenhouse which housed my aunt's pet cacti and other fascinating shrubs and plants. In a moment, I was on the wall and after those luscious looking plums!

Unfortunately, they were just out of my reach, and in order to pluck them, I had to stretch quite a bit which would tend to make me overbalance. I accordingly did a very foolish thing. With the weight of my body on the wall at the back, I thought that a momentary slight pressure with one foot on the greenhouse as I leaned forward, would do the trick. There was a loud crack, but I acted like lightning, and without realising it found myself actually leaping across the top of the conservatory, breaking pane after pane of glass, until I fell headlong through the rest!

There was a dreadful splintering crash. The silence which followed was ominous, and my brother, waiting for me to throw down the plums, thought I had been killed. Extricating myself with difficulty (which added to the process of destruction) I jumped down to survey the wreckage. It was nothing short of tragic. My aunt had just spent a considerable amount of time and money on renovations, and now see what I had done! The newly painted greenhouse looked a sorry mess indeed.

We slowly made our way to the lawn, hidden from the house by the shrubbery, and sat there for some time before we could pluck up enough courage to return and report on the situation. This was the hardest part. To make matters worse, with only a few scratches I could expect little sympathy. Why wasn't my leg hanging off? Why did I have to make such a mess without any blood to show for it? My clothes weren't even torn in the process!

Well, the inevitable happened! When they discovered I wasn't even hurt, I clearly remember the consequences! But it was my Grannie's words that I will never forget. I can hear them to this day. She was a wonderful Christian woman, and totally blind for the last twenty years of her life. She said, "Bob never does things by halves. He will either go flat out for God or for the devil. Make no mistake about that." Those words rang in my ears . . . *"He will either go flat out for God or for the devil."*

I wasn't a Christian then, at least not by Bible standards, for I certainly wasn't born again. It was always my nature to do things thoroughly. No one else could have demolished a newly renovated conservatory so effectively, and my father paid for the consequences in hard cash. It was several years later that I found Christ as my Saviour, and I am sure that Grannie was right. I have analysed the situation many times, and firmly believe that if I wasn't a Christian, I would most certainly have been an out-and-out child of the devil. There is something about the whole of my 'make-up' which would have been conducive to this end, something perhaps wonderful in Christian experience, but deadly otherwise. Let me share some of these things with you, indicating that often the most unlikely people can become useful Christians.

Maybe you are decisive, a very important trait in Christian character, for to dilly-dally about anything is often a great hindrance to spiritual growth. Indecisive people run the risk of breakdown, leaving others to make up their minds for them instead of acting for themselves. On the other hand decisive people do make a number of wrong decisions, but the Lord always graciously over-rules and brings blessing as He examines the motives behind such decisions. Just think of the mess some of us would have made of our lives if we had made important decisions without God! Being quick off the mark, we could have married the wrong person or decided upon the wrong ambition. We could have embarked upon a wrong business transaction or become gamblers, if not at the races, possibly on the Stock Exchange. Yes, thank God that many of us did not go flat out for the devil in making quick decisions.

Some of us are by nature loving people, admittedly not lovely ones, but capable of loving. Without Christ we could have wrecked our lives and the lives of others through infatuation or unfaithfulness. As it is, the Lord gives us such wonderful love for our life partners that all this is gloriously safeguarded, and we seek to bring up our families in the shelter of such love. In this way our children make their own personal commitment to Christ and love us in return. We still have to be very careful not to allow such love to become possessive or selfish, for Christ said *"He that loveth father or mother, son or daughter, more than Me, is not worthy of Me."* When our capacity for human love is transformed into divine love, it never becomes lust, which is the perversion of the real thing.

Many of us have a tremendous capacity for thirst. I know from my own experience how easily I perspire after a few minutes in the garden, and can readily consume gallons of liquid refreshment. What would this mean to some of us if we were not converted? Maybe our natural thirst would have turned us into habitual drunkards or worse? Yes, my Grannie was right: *"He will either go flat out for God or for the devil."* Then what about those of us who have a real taste for adventure? My wife and I have been around the world several times, yet we wonder what might have happened had we not been committed Christians. The worldly atmosphere and the wickedness as well could readily have lured us into permissiveness if we had not known the Lord. Oh yes, life would have been so different, and our adventures would have led many of us into disillusionment and despair instead of creating opportunities for leading people to the Lord.

Outspokeness is also a trait of many of the Lord's people, and this has got me into hot water at times! Just think of the hardness of heart that could result from a hasty critical attitude on this level without Christ. It could readily cut us off from all our friends. Our keen perception of right and wrong could have led us into all kinds of social and political upheavals. As it is, the Lord has seen fit to use a forthright ministry in these days of watered-down truths, and we are so glad to be out and out for Him and not for the devil.

Yes, the experience of smashing my Grannie's greenhouse while attempting to steal plums off the tree next door has taught me some great lessons. Naturally I have not forgotten the incident which was highlighted by the wise old lady's remark . . . Don't you think she was right?

2   Cross Roads

This is the way, walk ye in it.

(Isa. 30: 21)

Some years ago I read a good interpretation of those
biblical words, *"Many are called but few chosen."* It
went something like this . . . many are called, but
few choose to avail themselves of the call.

I think this is fairly accurate because God calls all
His children into some form of service. The insignificant housewife whose vision is no wider than the kitchen
sink can be called of God to be of immense value to
the Lord. Likewise, the big businessman whose life
may be swamped by earthly investments is called to
give an account of his stewardship as he dedicates his
profits to God's service. The factory worker, the nurse
at the hospital, the school teacher, the busy secretary,
all are called to be witnesses to Him. Many are called,
but few even hear the call . . . there are too many
other voices clamouring for attention.

With regard to the call to foreign lands, I have come
to regard this not as something special but as a priority
call. Many times the question is asked . . . "Have you
had the call?" Just pause for a moment. What is meant
by that question? The Lord has already sounded it
forth in these words . . . *"Go ye into all the world and
preach the Gospel to every creature."* That's pretty
clear isn't it? I don't think there is anything special
about that as far as you and I are concerned. The
under-privileged nations—those who have never heard
the Gospel—surely claim our attention. I would suggest
that the question should be phrased differently. Not

14

"Have you *had* the call?", but "Have you *heard* the call?"

"But surely," you argue, "not all can go to the foreign mission field, for some are not educated, others would break down in health, and there must certainly be pastors, teachers and Christian workers in the homeland as well?" That is perfectly true. However, if Christians realised it was God's special call to stay at home, and accepted the challenge of world evangelism at its face value, the situation would be very different from what it is today.

My wife and I recently visited Japan, and we were reminded that General McArthur begged for ten thousand missionaries of the Cross to take up the challenge at the end of the war. The Japanese people were frustrated, bewildered, defeated, and ready to grasp at anything. What an opportunity for the Gospel. Yet, only a handful of missionaries responded, just a few hundred, if that. And the consequence? Today Japan is a well-ordered, efficient country with an economy which almost guarantees the equivalent of several hundred pounds in everybody's bank account. Who wants spiritual help when materialism abounds?

It is accurate to say that the church has lost its most valuable opportunity for evangelism in that great land. Why? Because Christians thought they had to have a special call to leave all and follow the Master. McArthur's plea fell on deaf ears. The Lord's people were too busy collecting their spoils, and getting rehabilitated to peace time conditions at home, to hear the challenge.

Today, doors of opportunity in many countries which were once wide open are fast closing. Passports and visas are more difficult to obtain than ever before. Naturally this gives us a glorious opportunity for an effective radio ministry to many lands, and we see the hand of God in raising up this means of mass communication, but it is also an indictment on the

15

Christian church for failing to rise up and follow the universal call to missionary service. Now we are reaping the consequences. Many of the Lord's people are becoming materialistic, and their children are subsequently not interested in missions any more. One of the saddest things today is the decline in numbers attending missionary rallies, for many young people seem more interested in Christian entertainment than in Christian enterprise.

But how does one hear the call? Is there a special way in which we can be tuned in to the right wavelength? You know it is only when we set out to discover His will that we distinctly hear a voice behind us saying, *"This is the way, walk ye in it."* Of course there must be the willingness to do His will at all costs before direction is given. This is most important. If we are set on doing our will and determined to plan our own lives as Christians we will never hear His voice. The only time many of us are likely to look for guidance is when things go wrong, and often things go wrong because we have not purposefully set our sights in His direction.

A word of personal testimony might help. Years ago, as a young businessman, I had the great desire to buy up every opportunity of witnessing of the Lord. This was not detrimental to my career, but rather enhanced it. In fact I was promoted for unusual success! I soon learned how important it was not to pressurise anyone into making a decision. It had to come about in a perfectly natural way in the course of business, or not at all. Naturally such a desire is back of all true missionary enterprise, and it was not long before the clear recognition came that those who had never heard the Gospel in other lands had the priority claim. However the Lord had to show me the real value of materialistic gain before He could break through in this direction. When I saw the worthlessness of it all, I fell on my knees under a tree in a Cheshire lane and dedicated my life to whatever He might have planned for me—anywhere! I knew I was at the crossroads.

I was now subsequently "in the way" and thus tuned in to hear His voice. It surely came. I saw a placard outside a shop with the words: "The Present Situation in India." At the time it hardly registered, but God was working. A day or two later I received two letters in the mail, one from my mother in the south of England and the other from my fiancée in the north. Both had been to missionary meetings and had listened to the Lord's servants from India. Then I was invited by my old friend, Mr. Hudson Pope, to attend a missionary rally in Harrogate. Imagine my surprise when the speaker was a Miss Peggy Lang from India. The next night at the Baptist Church, the speaker was a missionary from South America; he suddenly looked straight at me in the balcony and spoke on the needs of India. When I returned to my lodgings some miles away, the first thing my landlady said to me was, "We had a visitor to lunch today . . . a missionary from India"!

Why India? My fiancée was born in India, the daughter of a Government official, and she had since been gloriously converted at a students' campaign in Edinburgh. Was the Lord calling her back to that land in another capacity. I wondered, but not for long.

I was transferred to Hoylake in the Wirral, Cheshire, and a few days later visited Kingsmead School to find a missionary hymn of India staring me in the face as I strummed on the piano. A day or two later, while visiting a doting patient, I was shown a children's book in which his little daughter had recently published a poem. As he proudly exhibited this to me, I hardly noticed it. On the other page in glaring headlines, I read, "Adventures in India". I simply could not get away from India. Moreover, for several days on my "Cheering Words" calendar by my bedside I had been

17

reading missionary texts. There was no doubt that God was speaking.

The pressure became so great that I decided to shut myself in with the Lord until I was sure that He was calling me to India. On my knees I read from Isaiah chapter sixty: *"Arise, shine for thy light is come."* How much I needed light just then. "Oh Lord," I prayed, "Please show me Thy will." I was led to refer to chapty forty, verse six, as I looked up "light" in the reference margin. Then it was I read those words which were especially for me and for me alone on that particular occasion . . . *"I the Lord have called thee."* The words stood out as if illuminated in a special way. I was overwhelmed by His presence and just worshipped. Then it was that I tore off the calendar for the day and much to my amazement read a text from Esther which actually spoke of India — the only verse in the whole of the Bible mentioning this great continent: *"The posts rode from India."* The matter was settled. I must resign immediately. I did so, and a few years later set sail for India with a young wife who was also assured of God's call for her. And when His purpose in that part of the world was completed, He led us to work amongst the Indians in the Fiji Islands.

Not every missionary is given such a clear confirmation of his or her call. Sometimes the need of a certain country is brought clearly to mind, although the "need", which is universal, never constitutes the call. There is as much need at home as there is abroad, and often friends and relatives subtly remind us of this to dissuade us from going overseas! We must first be willing to do anything, or go anywhere, in fact to have dealings with God until He brings us to this place of willingness. The rest is over to Him and He will not fail to point out His will by saying at the crossroads, *"This is the way, walk ye in it."* He may say something like that to you and to me today.

3   Skilful Hands

*He guided them by the skilfulness of
his hands.*   (Psa. 78:72)

My wife and I have shared many wonderful experiences
and I am sure the following incident will indicate the
skilfulness of our Lord's hands in what might otherwise seem a small and insignificant detail.

We were in India at the time, and we felt that it was
necessary for us to make a break from the organisation
with which we were associated, in order to further the
Lord's interests in another direction.

We knew that the Lord had been leading us for
some time to take action, but humanly speaking almost
everything seemed against us. It was war time, and to
forego a measure of regular financial support by our
resignation was not an attractive proposition. We were
also expecting another addition to the family, and
moreover the whole thing was against the advice of
most of our fellow missionaries who urged us to remain
with the organisation until such a time as we returned
home on furlough.

However, we could not get away from the strong
insistence of the Holy Spirit to move by faith in entire
dependence upon the Lord. There was also the matter
of returning to the Mission a certain sum which had
been contributed towards outgoing expenses, not much
in this world's estimation, but a vast amount to us . . .
about £20 in all. If the Lord was urging us to take this
step, no doubt He would provide this requirement. It
seemed humanly impossible in the light of the fact that
we had been living on roughly £7 a month, but He is

faithful, and we just left matters in His good hands.

The final decision had to be made at the annual conference when all the missionaries gathered together at our headquarters in Hyderabad State. The matter of our pending resignation was on the agenda for discussion, and we made the journey by road in fear and trepidation. What would the outcome be? We knew that we were considered foolish in leaving the shelter of a faith organisation for a life of entire dependence on the Lord, especially on the mission field and in war time. I was strongly advised to reconsider the possible consequences for my wife and family in the light of her expectancy. Would I be prepared to sell tea for my support? I was firm in my reply, that if the Lord was leading us into another sphere of service then He would adequately care for all our needs besides. It seemed foolhardy and ridiculous, but I was convinced of this. The big question was . . . "What is His will?"

At the first meeting we were almost electrified to learn that through the kindness of certain supporters, some back "allowances" were to be distributed to each missionary, and our share totalled the *exact* sum owing to the Mission if we were to sever our connection. How amazing! It was just what we had earnestly prayed for as a seal to our outgoing involvement.

We drove to Secunderabad city with the cheque in order to draw the cash in settlement, and also to do some necessary shopping, with the calm assurance that the money had been sent by the Lord as His seal of approval. My wife eventually tucked the bank notes into her handbag to bring back with us to the conference.

On the way back, near the outskirts of the city, we discovered to our great consternation that she had mislaid her handbag. We stopped the car and made a thorough search, but to no avail. It had gone! Someone must have stolen it! We went hot and cold all over.

20

It wasn't so much the financial loss that shook us, but the fact that this had been God's seal on our future movements. What could we say now? Perhaps He didn't want us to take this decisive step, and yet everything else pointed to it so clearly. We were positively baffled. After a thorough search in the dark there was certainly no sign of the handbag in the car, and we were almost resigned to the situation. There were matters of principle involved, and if you knew all the details, all the heartaches, and all the tears over many months of agonising before the Lord, the loss of this handbag meant more to us than anything else in the world at that moment. Our positive declarations of faith and deepest inward convictions would completely disappear with the loss of that bag. What was the meaning of it all? We almost wept with anguish. To expect to find it in an Indian bazaar was impossible. Whatever had happened, it was now irretrievable. Some fortunate Indian was rejoicing in his find and two unfortunate missionaries were almost beside themselves with inner conflict.

Suddenly my wife gave a cry, "Bob, here it is", and scarcely believing my ears I followed her gaze to the running board of that old vehicle. There was the bag containing the money balanced precariously on the very edge. A few more bumps, and we would have lost it forever in the deep ruts of an Indian cartway, but it was safe. Yes, it had been placed on the board by my wife when we had called at a garage some miles back and she had forgotten all about it. The amazing thing was how it had remained there during the bumpy ride over the past few miles of cart tracks. It was a miracle!

Instantly our doubts gave place to a tremendous sense of assurance. If the Lord could keep an old handbag on the edge of a running board over rough Indian roads, He could certainly keep us as a family in the hollow of His hands, no matter what lay ahead!

"Thank you Lord," we breathed. Reverently retrieving the bag, we knew full well that He wanted us to make the break no matter the consequences, and this was gloriously justified by Him later on.

But it was when we got back that we received further wonderful confirmation from the Lord through a fellow missionary who was thoroughly sympathetic with our deep exercise of heart. This is what Les Carter said: "The Lord has been speaking very definitely to me concerning your future and He has given me a verse for you." We were staggered when he read to us from Psalm 78:72 . . . *"He guided them by the skilfulness of His hands."* How wonderful! When we told him the story of the handbag, he fully understood. Only the Lord's skilful hands could have kept that bag on the edge of the running board, and it was a further confirmation of our decision to make the move.

I think the climax came when we missionaries each took a customary "promise" out of a box as it was passed around during our final meal together. How we breathed that we might be given a *public* seal on our tremendous decision! When my wife read hers, the silence could be felt . . . *"Ye shall go out with joy and be led forth with peace."* When my turn came, it was again obvious that the Lord had been working . . . *"The Holy Spirit shall teach you in the same hour what ye ought to say",* and in my pocket was the letter of resignation to be delivered immediately afterwards!

Oh, how the Lord delights to confirm the steps of His servants all along the way! I am only too well aware that reliance upon promise boxes or texts at random from the Bible is a poor substitute for a complete dependence on the guiding hand of God and His Word, but there are times when He overrules in the ordinary everyday events of life, including the promise box. Here was an example!

So at this missionary conference, the money came to hand for the required agreement, preserved *"by the skilfulness of His hands"*, and promises were given in public to ratify the Lord's private dealings with us before our fellow missionaries. We left with complete confidence in Him to see us through, and He did wondrously . . . even providing us with a home in the Nilgiri Hills and all expenses paid at the nursing home, meeting every need besides, until He led us eventually to the next sphere of service in the Godavari Delta. How great is the God we adore!

Is there some problem relating to your future which must be faced today? Do so with every confidence in Him. If you are sure of His will, whatever the outcome may be, however difficult the road ahead, He will see you through. Remember, *"He guided them by the skilfulness of His hands."* This is the way He has always seen His people through, and He will not fail you. He saw us through those difficult days, even using His skilful hands to keep that precious handbag on the very edge of the running board to prevent it falling off. May you experience His keeping hand upon your life today.

4   Magic Words

First be reconciled to thy brother.
(Matt. 5: 24)

Some of the most forgotten sounds in today's vocabulary are the words . . . "I'm sorry". A number of young people have told me that they have never once heard their parents say them to anyone! What a difference they can make to a family, to a church, or to any group of people. Surely if we obey God's Word and love one another, these words shouldn't be too difficult to say? I firmly believe that the world would be transformed if all God's children learned to say them and to mean them today.

Quite a number of years ago I began to learn one of the greatest lessons in Christian discipleship, particularly involving those important relationships with fellow believers in Christ. My whole attitude in this direction has never been quite the same since, and one humbling experience taught me a great lesson. *"By this shall all men know that ye are my disciples, if ye have love one to another."*

We were on the mission field in India, seeking to serve the Lord in the midst of numerous hardships and difficulties. Through privation, loneliness and the general climatic conditions, to say nothing of the "care of the churches", the pressure was on. We had also buried our first baby daughter and little realised that we were to pass through a similar fiery test before many more days, but in the meanwhile we were planning an evangelistic itinerary in a number of villages surrounding the Godavari Delta. For this purpose we were graciously loaned a houseboat by a fellow missionary in order to spend a week or two in the many villages along the banks of the canal area.

We accordingly prepared to take our children with us, and an Indian servant was responsible for the general upkeep of the houseboat. I had given strict orders that the boat was to be thoroughly washed and disinfected owing to the ravages of infectious diseases such as dysentery, typhoid, and cholera, which are easily picked up through germ-laden dust and dirt.

Imagine my concern when I discovered that he had not done his job properly and we were to embark upon our evangelistic tour in a filthy boat. I am very much afraid that for the moment I was livid. Pointing out the situation to this careless man I lost my temper, and seizing him by his shirt actually tore it in my anger. It all took place in a moment of time before I could realise what had happened. And then the consequences!

I realised in a flash that as far as my ministry was concerned, it was finished. This man would never listen to me again. Moreover, he would most certainly make a big thing of it before the Christian community, and my reputation was already down the drain. I *had* to do something about it, and something quickly. I heard voices.

One whispered, "Get alone with the Lord and ask for His forgiveness." That would have been easy. I could have fled to the privacy of my study and wept if necessary before God. But in the meantime the man would have gone away with a big grudge in his heart.

Another voice said, "Buy him a new shirt." I intended to do this in any case. It would certainly help, but would in no wise atone for the wrong done. It would have been my duty, that's all, and he would have fully expected it.

It was the still small voice that mattered most, and this voice said, *"If thou bring thy gift to the altar and*

25

there rememberest that thy brother hath ought against thee, first be reconciled to thy brother and then come and offer thy gift."

The Word of God shattered my shallow concepts of restitution. There was no cost attached to a private confession, and little financial outlay in buying a new shirt . . . but the awful price involved in getting right with my brother hurt my pride. Humanly speaking I would rather buy him a dozen new shirts than say sorry! Many reasonable arguments rose up against obeying this still small voice. Didn't I pay him to do the job? Hadn't he failed miserably? Shouldn't he be reprimanded? Were we not likely to pick up deadly germs as a result? Wasn't I responsible for the well-being of my family? Incidentally, we did succumb to the ravages of disease during the subsequent trip, for shortly afterwards my wife was desperately ill with typho-malaria, Peter almost died with dysentry, and our darling little Joy was actually taken Home as a result. But I can never blame this man for such a strange turn of events as these things could have eventuated from any village we visited on that tour.

I stood there in front of him, my hand still firm on his shoulders as many conflicting thoughts passed through my mind. Then I just looked up and prayed, "Lord, help me." The next minute I simply said, "I'm sorry brother, please forgive me." It wasn't easy, but by the grace of God it was accomplished. I had at least obeyed.

The result was electrifying. The man instantly fell to his knees and started to confess many sins to the Lord that I never dreamed were hidden away in his life. He cried like a baby and in a few minutes we were both kneeling before the Throne of Grace with our arms around each other . . . true brothers in Christ. The miracle had taken place. We were reunited in a new way. There was love in our hearts that was Divine, and I never had a more faithful employee. The fact that

26

we were real brothers in Christ eclipsed everything else, and moreover my preaching, instead of being ruined, became more effective than ever. No wonder we faced such a fiery trial afterwards!

There is so much we can learn from this experience. So much I have learned at any rate. It is always best to keep short accounts with our Christian brothers and sisters so that the ground is clear of all roots of bitterness that otherwise encumber the pathway we tread. I believe it is more important to say "I'm sorry" than it is to take any prominent place in Christian activity . . . for unless we do this whenever necessary (and a few experiences certainly help to prevent embarrassing recurrences!), we will never win the lost to Christ. I know some Christians who have actually knocked on their unconverted neighbour's door and sought forgiveness for their lack of concern with amazing results. Others have asked their work-mates to forgive them for their poor Christian testimony. It's never easy, but miracles take place when we respond to the "still, small voice" in this way.

You see, the world around us is not looking for the perfect Christian, for it would look in vain. The world is searching for the Christian who is willing to admit his faults and failures when called upon to do so. This is a down to earth reality, although I believe with all my heart that Christ can give us complete victory over all known sin. He could have given me the victory over my hasty temper before I tore my brother's shirt. I'm ready to admit that. But seeing that not one of us is perfect, and that at times we all give way to the flesh, we must also confess these faults to each other in order to prevent a repetition of the same kind of situation!

Don't think for one moment that I am condoning those deliberate and wilful sins which Christ condemns . . . we should have done with all these when we repented; but what I am emphasising it that certain 'urges' which come to all of us must be nipped in the

27

bud before the consequences ruin our testimony.

For example, the sex urge must be restrained before it develops into an infatuation or worse, and we may have to act promptly on this score. The bitter spirit must be removed before it develops into an impossible relationship. The casual concern for the lost must be repudiated before we become cold at heart. All these things and much more are latent in the hearts of the most saintly, and to deny their existence is to deceive ourselves, for victory over sin is only gloriously possible when we talk with the Lord and have dealings with Him, particularly in the light of true confession.

I suppose that if I had dealt graciously with my brother instead of tearing his shirt, it would have been far better, but having lost my temper I could have been tempted to leave it at that, which would have been ten times worse. I wonder if any of us will hear the still small voice speaking to us today . . . and if we do, what will our reaction be? Will we swallow our pride and say those few magic words . . . "I'm sorry"?

5 Jesuratnam's Confession

Bringing into captivity every thought.
(2 Cor. 10: 5)

The day promised to be a hot one. Rising early, we enjoyed what we could of the faint morning breeze, as we munched our breakfast or *chota*. Two boys arrived from the school while we were eating, and we were told that they had some confessions to make.

Looking out into the compound we saw one of them, a boy in whom we had great confidence and expectation, holding his head with real agony and conviction written all over his face. Our hearts sank. We had just had the painful experience of dismissing two young people from the school, such a promising couple too, especially the girl, and now the thought of further immorality coming to light was like a huge black cloud on the horizon of the dawn of a new day. Only those who know India will be able to enter into our feelings, for very few men escape immorality in the villages, and tremendous temptations are faced by young inexperienced Christians.

With great apprehension I went out to interview these young men. One confided matters of minor importance, and I dismissed him with forgiveness and a word of warning. Then I turned to the boy in question and hardly dared to open my mouth.

"Sir, I have committed a dreadful sin," he said, and then in a torrent of words, I caught the name of the sin I had dreaded to hear. I was overcome, that looking sadly into his face all I could say was, "Jesuratnam" (which means "Jesus' precious stone") "I am grieved beyond measure. I cannot talk with you now, but come back again at four o'clock." I left him and took the matter to the Lord with a heavy heart. Was not Jesuratnam one of the most promising boys in the school? Had he not left home without his clothing to escape from the clutches of his heathen parents? Had he not rescued his little sister from a life of unspeakable shame bringing her to the school and beseeching us to take her in? Was he not one of our brightest boys? Oh, the unspeakable horror of it all! It seemed that the Lord was deserting us.

At four o'clock in the afternoon, Jesuratnam turned turned up to see me. I called him into the bungalow, and we found a quiet corner where we could chat together. Oh, how ashamed he was! Then I began to show him from the Word of God the awfulness of such a sin, that God in His love was bound to punish such a person, and that it produced unutterable bondage and misery. He nodded in agreement. I then mentioned how grieved I was to think that he had fallen such a prey to Satan in this way.

After a long discourse he broke in . . . "But Sir, I did not commit the sin outwardly. The great desire came over me with such overwhelming force that I had to flee from the house in order to overcome it." I could hardly believe my ears, but the radiant look in his face told me he was telling the truth.

"Yes, Sir. I did not stop until I got here. I knew I would be safe in the Bible School and now I long for God to deliver me from these dreadful temptations." We knelt together and as he asked the Lord's forgiveness for allowing the sinful desires to arise, he also praised God for having kept him from the act, and pleaded that all such desires be completely cleansed from his heart.

What a burden rolled off my shoulders. I would have been saved from much travail of soul that day had I listened carefully to his words in the morning. The difference between grammatical and colloquial Telugu is such that extra care must be exercised by beginners in listening to every word spoken.

I dismissed him and with great joy told him to witness to his fellow students as to how the Lord had been dealing with him. He went off with a beaming face, radiant with the joy of the Lord. That the heart of a young man only a short time saved from Hindu darkness should be so sensitive to the things of God is nothing short of a miracle, but then of course this is the work of our heavenly Father, and what we are to expect. That night our hearts sang praises to Him for this triumph of His grace.

Well this story of Jesuratnam causes us to reflect upon our present society with alarm. Little did we realise that in such a short time, our own nation would be involved in so much permissiveness. The sin which Jesuratnam had committed in his heart as a Christian is now being committed by so-called Christians openly. Immorality, which ran rife in India, now overwhelms *us*. Our own nation, once renowned for her integrity, is now famed for her immorality, and where do we go from here?

Jesuratnam, this young Indian convert, so new in the Christian faith, was convicted of harbouring sinful thoughts and came to confess them with the object of being delivered. How wonderful! "Sir," he said, "I have committed a dreadful sin." I do not believe that we Christians will ever regain our power and authority before men until the Holy Spirit brings us to this place of deep conviction within. Its the THOUGHT LIFE that needs cleansing.

It has been my experience to counsel hundreds of men and women who only get troubled over sin when they have committed the act, and then I believe it is often far too late to avoid the calamitous involvements. On every hand today the thought life of our community is being brain-washed with satanic intrigue.

31

Every available means of reducing sin to the level of an accepted permissible standard of living is being exploited by mass media including the press, radio, and television.

Sin is no longer sin, even to some evangelical Christians. It's becoming just a matter of how you look at things. Extra-marital or pre-marital relationships are not necessarily wrong, depending on the circumstances. So the thought life is no longer sensitive to the will and mind of a holy and righteous God. The word "fornication" has almost disappeared from our vocabulary as being too offensive, and if the Christian sins immorally, there is often no real conviction or repentance. It will all work out satisfactorily in the long run, so they say.

Oh, what an indictment on a situation which thirty years ago would have brought even the unconverted to their knees! Where do we find someone like Jesuratnam, crying out before God, "I have committed a dreadful sin," when it only involves the thought life?

Yes, it is the thought life of an individual that shapes the social life of a community. *"As a man thinketh in his heart, so is he."* If the danger of today's educational system is that it takes no account of man's sin, then the danger of today's evangelical outlook is that it cheapens God's forgiveness. Jesuratnam feared the consequences of wrong and evil and fled from the scene before he was overcome. Today, evangelicals often sink deep into the mire of sin before they begin to fear the consequences. The result is catastrophic! The lowering of spiritual standards is inevitable. Jesuratnam thought before he acted . . . today men act before they have thought.

The Bible declares that the Christian must *"bring into captivity every thought to the obedience of Christ",* and this is perhaps the greatest need of the hour. We cannot think properly unless we have the mind of Christ, and we cannot have the mind of Christ

32

unless we give heed to His Word. The greatest sin of this generation must go down in history as total disregard for the Word of God.

Jesuratnam, an ignorant young Hindu convert, was convicted of sin within his thought life because he was studying God's Word. God's Word declares sin to be sin. God's Word declares . . . *"Out of the heart proceed evil thoughts,"* and *"The thoughts of the wicked are an abomination."* It was because of this that Jesuratnam knew the mind of God when his thoughts turned to evil. He did not wait until his wicked desires were fulfilled to see what would happen, as many do today. Like Joseph, he fled from the scene, crying from his heart, *"How can I do this great wickedness and sin against God?"*

If Jesuratnam had fallen a prey to his sinful desires, what might have happened? Well, that's anybody's guess, but it is possible that his little sister would have gone back to her life of wickedness, perceiving no difference between her past sins and her brother's! It is possible that his parents might never have been converted, seeing no radical change in their son's attitude to sin. This happens again and again. Joseph would never have become Prime Minister of Egypt, that's for sure, if he had sinned with Potiphar's wife . . . so you see, it does make a difference. Sin in your life and mine damns others. Let us pray therefore that our attitude to sin, like Jesuratnam's, will have a profound effect upon somebody's life today before it is too late. Remember, God's Word will keep you from sin or else sin will keep you from God's Word!

6   Train Journey

That they might have life. (John 10: 10)

The train gathered momentum as it sped through the Somerset countryside. It was a glorious summer day and the sun, filtering through the wispy cotton wool clouds, formed a continuous shifting pattern on the vivid rolling green fields.

The atmosphere was one of relaxation, and most travellers were making themselves comfortable for a quiet, pleasant journey. The only person in my compartment was a man buried in his newspaper. He wasn't even interested in talking about the weather—always a good subject in the UK—and when he left the train at the next station I was alone.

Feeling sure that the Lord intended me to make a contact on that journey, I left my seat to explore the situation by a walk along the corridor. There might be some likely prospects in another part of the train!

Sure enough, in the very next compartment I saw two young men in khaki looking the picture of misery. Their only companion was a clergyman. I put two and two together and thought of a plan. Returning to my seat I began to pray for guidance. Should I burst into the compartment next door and begin a conversation with the clergyman on spiritual matters? If he was a born-again Christian, those fellows would hear the Gospel in no uncertain way . . . but if he was just religious, they would get an ear-full anyway. What should I do? I felt the opportunity was too great to miss. "Lord, please help thy servant," I pleaded.

I didn't have long to wait. As I was praying, I heard the click of the sliding door indicating that someone was about to join me. I looked up, and to my amazement saw the two young soldiers entering my compartment. It was astounding! How speedily my request had been answered. Truly it was one of the quickest answers to prayer I could ever remember.

"What brings you fellows into my compartment in the middle of a journey?" I asked.

"Oh, him," one of them indicated, referring to the clergyman with a jerk of his thumb. "He's too good and religious for us!"

The humour of the situation gripped me and I could hardly restrain from laughing. Quite obviously the gentleman next door was going to be mild in their estimation compared to me. I don't think he had even opened his mouth to say anything, whereas I was ready with the Gospel. Pretending to sympathise with them I showed complete agreement with their attitude towards religion, which in any case was mine.

"Quite right," I said. "Religion has never helped anybody. I was once religious myself, but it never got me anywhere." We were getting on fine.

"Sure," one of them agreed as he flung his haversack on the rack and settled back for an easy time. "We've had enough of religion in the army."

As they adjusted to their new situation congratulating themselves that they were now out of a religious environment I suddenly threw out a challenge.

"As a matter of fact, you don't realise that I happen to be a preacher of the Gospel," I said.

They looked spellbound, positively spellbound. It seemed quite a time before one of them said, "Help, I'm going to sleep." The other one's eyes were open so wide that he couldn't possibly shut them if he had tried. This was my golden opportunity and I took it without hesitation.

"Listen, chaps. There's a great difference between

35

religion and reality. The man next door might be religious, but he might not have the goods. You see, Christ never came to make people religious humbugs. He spoke more scathing words about hypocrisy than anyone else, and it was the religous crowd that hounded him to death. He came to bring LIFE. The kind you fellows are craving for and haven't managed to find. You've tried almost everything and failed. It's the kind of life you need, and He will give it to you. Listen to what He says, *'I am come that they might have life, and have it more abundantly.'* "

By this time, the fellow who said he was going to sleep was not only awake, he was actually sitting next to me looking into the pages of my New Testament to verify the truth for himself. It was an unforgettable experience, but my heart was thrilled when they told me of a chap billeted with them who was unafraid to kneel at his bedside before retirement. I could well imagine one of his prayers being answered right then and there in that railway compartment. We had a tremendous time together talking about the things of the Lord, and before they got out at Exeter, they both gave me the greatest handshake I had ever had, while I slipped a tract into the other. I was wincing for some time afterwards!

God has wonderful purposes of reinforcing the truth of redemption in the most unusual way if we let Him. I am sure we are never meant to embarrass anyone unnecessarily in front of others, although they will rarely feel awkward in our presence when alone with us. To shout texts in buses, and to hand out tracts indiscriminately could frighten more people away from Christ than win any to Him. There is a time and season for everything, and people do regard a measure of privacy as being essential in this direction. I can recount times when whole groups of people have shared spiritual things in a place like a railway compartment, but it is always spontaneous and without necessarily handing out tracts to everyone. These two young men were alone when they were challenged, with no one to back them up or to take my side. It left them helpless, yet unembarrassed. It was prepared ground for an attack.

I well remember taking another journey on an Indian train when a Brahmin, recognising that I was a missionary, challenged me outright in front of many other passengers in a large open railway carriage. Squatting on the luggage rack above me, the favourite position for opening out your bedding, he looked down and said, "Sahib, all religions lead to the same place. This train is going to Calcutta, but there are many trains from all parts of India going to the same city, and they will all get there in the end. So it is with religion. You Westerners have the Christian religion. We are Hindus. We will arrive at the same place in the end! "

It sounded so plausible. His argument was very convincing. He had everyone on his side. All were nodding their heads in agreement. I thought I would take him up on his own ground.

"You believe there is virtually no difference in the religious systems of the world?" I asked. He nodded assent.

"Well then," I continued, "Please tell everyone in this compartment that you have absolutely no objection to your son becoming a Christian because it really makes no difference at all! "

The old man was taken unawares. To admit this before his Hindu companions would be to sanction Christianity, which he could never do at any price. He saw the folly of his own statement and perhaps a glimmer of light as well, and this gave me the opportunity I was waiting for. As I testified to the claims of Christ and what He had done for me, I had quite an attentive hearing. There is no embarrassment in talking about spiritual things in India, and it is the same message to the same needy hearts about the same

Saviour everywhere. Maybe God will give you unusual opportunities of witnessing for the Lord today. Keep your eyes open, but do not create embarrassment.

I remember a young man who had just been discharged from the army, entering a railway compartment and sitting next to me full of exuberance at his release. He began singing out loud some pop songs he himself had composed, and everyone was on his side. Presently I quietly drew from my pocket a chorus I had set to music and asked if he could sing it to us. It only occurred to him after he had started off just what was involved, but he had to sing it through! I can see the impact on everyone to this day. If I had tried to sing it . . . what a flop and failure . . . but to get him to do it was altogether different. Almost everyone took part in the conversation which followed.

On another occasion I was so full of the joy of the Lord after a wonderful meeting that when I got into the train which was crowded, I took a crying baby from a frustrated mother, and sat her on my knee. This got them all on my side and subsequent witnessing without embarrassment was easy.

Surely, *"I am come that they might have life."* Do you possess that life today or are you just religious?

7   Wasting Time

*Redeeming the time, because the days
are evil.*   (Eph. 5: 16)

It was a cold clear night with a touch of frost. Winter
was around the corner and I had just had a very encouraging meeting in Crewkerne, Somerset. Driving
back home to Bath in the brilliant moonlight, I thought
how different it was from a few months earlier in
India, when we were enduring dreadful heat, avoiding
clouds of mosquitoes and drinking tepid boiled water!
Wrapping my overcoat around my legs I thanked the
Lord for providing this little car for use during our
short stay in England. As I planted my foot more
firmly on the accelerator, impatient to get home to
be with my wife and family, I thought how wonderful
it was to be on furlough, although it was certainly not
proving a rest by any stretch of imagination!

I had just parked the car in a rented garage near
the missionary home in St. Luke's Road, and was
closing the doors when the vehicle gave a sudden lurch
and fell to one side. The bracket holding one of the
kingpins had fractured, causing the front wheel to
come off! My, what an escape! Supposing this had
happened a few minutes before, when I was travelling
at speed? I shuddered at the thought, and as I made
my way home I gave thanks to God for a wonderful
deliverance.

Now repair bills have a nasty way of making themselves known just when you don't seem to have the

necessary cash to pay for them. I had been stung before, and this time I thought I would effect the repairs myself. I accordingly ordered the spare parts, and when they arrived, proceeded with a tool box to the garage to spend the morning as a mechanic.

But do you think I could shift that old kingpin out of its socket? With my hammer I hit it again and again from every conceivable angle, but it just wouldn't budge. In our morning devotions that day we had read from Job . . . *"Man is born unto trouble as the sparks fly upward."* Believe me there was plenty of trouble! One particularly hefty blow saw not only sparks but sent a small chip of metal bouncing off my cheek into the eyeball. I think I still have the mark to this day.

A woman shopper passing by saw my dilemma as I tried to remove the obstacle with an oily rag. She graciously wiped my eye of blood, and delicately retrieved the offending splinter of steel with her nice clean handkerchief. I must have presented quite a formidable sight, covered with smears of grease and blood, but there was no point in pretending to continue as a qualified mechanic. I went home to lunch, and afterwards made my way to our local garage, requesting a mechanic's help.

It all seemed so easy. The garage hand just looked at it for a few seconds, and then "ping", out it came with the first deft blow. I had hit it for hours on end without success! It's the "know-how" you pay for, so I learned! I was able to finish the job and returned home to find Leith Samuel and his wife who had just dropped in to see us. I will never forget how Leith laughed and laughed when I told him what I had been doing that morning. But there was something he said which I have never forgotten, something I have found to be sound advice indeed.

As he was doubling up with laughter, he suddenly said, "Fancy the Lord's servant trying to save the Lord's money and wasting the Lord's time!"

I have learned that there are many things that cannot be paid for in cash, and that one of the most valuable commodities for the Lord's servant is TIME. I firmly believe that if a number of missionary societies and churches, instead of looking to see how economically a project could be run, thought in terms of time instead, they would get much more in return for an investment well above their conservative estimate. It seems to me that a venture of faith involving thousands of pounds is more important to God than no venture at all because a committee cannot think of paying for it!

There are many niggardly aspects with respect to God's work which has greatly suffered as a result. Here in the UK, the missionary has been regarded in the past as someone who can sleep in the attic; someone who would be glad of everything second-best and second-rate; someone who can do with an old wreck of a car, if he needs one at all, and so much of our giving has been limited to jumble sales and missionary boxes. If every Christian gave the Lord the equivalent of what an unconverted person spends on drinks and tobacco, there would be no need to be miserly in our Gospel outreach. The One who owns the cattle on a thousand hills is the One who delights to meet the needs of His servants, whether the need be a few pence or a few thousand pounds. This may involve a good deal of sacrifice on the part of His people, but the principle remains the same. *"My God shall supply all your need according to His riches in glory by Christ Jesus."*

God is not stingy. Often an incentive to save the Lord's money is based upon a purely selfish desire to keep more of our own!

Time on the other hand, is a commodity that is becoming all too rare in these days. It is something that, once lost or wasted, can never be returned. Time to spend alone in the Lord's presence; time to witness

41

as the opportunity presents itself; time to study His Word; time for the prayer meeting; time to visit the sick. Yes, there seems to be little time for these things when endless hours in front of television never seem to be wasted! Have you not noticed that there is always plenty of time available in the midst of the busiest life to do exactly what we want to do?

My wife has just returned from a women's meeting to be told by the exasperated leader that many of the old ladies, mostly pensioners, spend all their time either attending meetings or playing bingo. They listen to the Gospel all right, but they seem much more interested in the cup of tea that follows. Even with nothing else to do, there is always plenty of time to pander to self rather than to seek God's will and do it. Yet, if asked to attend a prayer meeting or associate with a Gospel effort, the answer is invariably, "I haven't the time."

As a young man I well remember staying in lodgings on the outskirts of London with a woman who was very frugal in her manner of living. In a sense this was to be commended, but she never realised that in seeking to save a twopenny bus fare, she often wore out ten pennyworth of shoe leather!

Time is an expensive commodity these days. Every working hour in a man's life is worth a good deal of money. We have to face the fact that labour charges amount to considerably more than the cost of materials in most cases. Yet do we see that the Lord's servants are given their share in terms of the time spent in preparation, travel and overtime? Do we realise that one hour's missionary meeting often involves a whole day's pay, and that a minimum gift must be equivalent to the basic wage claim? Yes, time is a much more important factor than money these days, especially when the cost of living is so high. To offer "expenses" in terms of petrol is an insult to the intelligence of a missionary when he has to pay road tax, insurance, repair bills, and spend hours of time in getting to and from his meetings. Maybe Leith Samuel's remark could apply to these situations. "Fancy the Lord's servants trying to save the Lord's money and wasting the Lord's time."

Yet I know of one person who could not bear to part with his money, but was always willing to help out with his time. He would do anything to help the servants of the Lord, but he held tightly to his money! He would offer to effect repairs, take people in his car, drive himself to the limit at all hours, except part with his money. This may be an exception, but maybe the truth could also apply to him . . . "the Lord's servant trying to save the Lord's money and wasting the Lord's time" on unnecessary repairs to the missionary's car when a cash gift would have fixed matters and given him a few extra hours for more important aspects of the Lord's work!

Let us ask the Lord to show us His guidance in this area of our Christian lives, that we may not waste time or money as we seek to do His will.

8   Bible or Science?

Let the redeemed of the Lord say so.
(Psa. 107: 2)

Some of you will have read the story of a young couple
who were our next-door neighbours in Southampton.
The details of their conversion made the background
for a previous "Gems of Grace" broadcast which was
also a chapter in the first "Gems of Grace" book.

Well I was clearing out some papers in the attic a
few days ago, when I came across this young man's
testimony which is so thoroughly up-to-date that I
felt it should be broadcast. It was originally handed to
my wife, who left it on the bedside table for me to read
when I returned from a meeting late one night.

You will remember that Doug and his wife were
an intelligent young couple who never darkened a
church building. They moved into the house next door
just a matter of days before we moved into our new
home. It was some time before a friendship was struck
up enabling us to strike the iron for Christ while it
was hot.

We refused to hand them tracts until confidence had
been established, as we wanted them to make the first
approach. We prayed that the opportunity would arise,
and in the story told, you heard all the interesting
details . . . about the loss of my wife's diamond from
her engagement ring, and how we took them to a
meeting when Doug resented the preacher, Mark
Kagan, and tore him to shreds before his face! Then
the deep conviction followed by their glorious conversion! It certainly is a wonderful story, but the

testimony which he left in the form of a letter to us both, is what I want to share with you now. It has appeared in print, and been broadcast over the air in other countries. It is quite a moving document, and you will have to forgive the personal element without which it would lack much of its intimacy. Here it is. I quote:

"My dear friends,

"As you are very much aware, Jo and I have recently had the tremendous joy of accepting Christ into our lives. The experience will always be one of my most treasured possessions, and now that I can see the event in something like its true perspective, I feel strongly that it should be recorded before the details grow dim. I can see now how all the events of my life led up to that thrilling climax which took place at midnight, on that tempestuous April night, when the Lord opened my eyes and showed me that it was not after all I who sat at the centre of the universe. Looking back I can see that, as a very small child, I almost knew Christ. I loved the story of the Cross, but I could not understand it, and there was no one to explain.

"We are born into an age of so-called popular science. This so-called science which is not science, says, 'Show me your figures and prove your formulae, and I will believe,' and we fall down and worship this science in a crazy temple of unrelated figures and mis-understood mumbo-jumbo founded upon an abyss of ignorance which is terrifying to contemplate. Is it therefore surprising that I turned my back on Christ and rejected the teaching of my Bible? I could find no scientific foundation for the events which the Bible recorded, and therefore I was compelled, perhaps a little reluctantly, to dismiss them as fables.

"With infinite conceit, I finally decided that the teaching of the Bible was an excellent thing for lesser intelligences than my own, but for my part it would suffice if I shaped my life to conform to the requirements of the ten commandments, or at least to a version of them suitably modified to suit the changed conditions of the age in which I lived. I managed to get along without Christ, I seldom went to church, and when I did I always managed to conceal my shame from myself with the aid of a large helping of science.

"The years of my adolescence passed by. I was selfish and self-centred to the nth degree, and yet somehow I managed also to be intensely and genuinely self-righteous. I set up my row of bright, twentieth-century idols and worshipped them. And I surveyed the wonderful creation that was me, and was greatly pleased; sometimes a little uneasy. There were occasional pauses in the unending round of pleasure-seeking when, in spite of myself, I would begin to wonder. But science was always around the corner to help. You can prove anything with figures. They are wonderful slaves; will do anything for you. Wonderful slaves and dreadful masters.

"Eventually the war came and I became hard and cynical. My back which had once been turned reluctantly on Christ was now turned resolutely. And yet, one night, I had to call on Christ, and although I had rejected Him, He did not fail me. I sat in a blazing aircraft plunging to destruction, completely powerless and petrified with fear, and from the depths of my tortured soul I called to Christ to help me. And I, who had scorned Christ, was plucked from the midst of that fiery furnace and delivered safely to the ground. And so base was my ingratitude that I did not even thank Him for it!

"In the two long years which followed, when I was a prisoner of war, I again forgot Christ. I forgot the One Who alone could have lifted me above the misery of those times. Whilst I was there, I learned much about my fellow men. I saw men reach great heights of nobility and great depths of selfish corruption, and

46

still I did not learn the lesson which was so plain before me.

"In the fulness of time I knew the great joy again of freedom. And what freedom! All that had happened was that the barbed wire had disappeared. I was still a prisoner, and my warder was the great insatiable me. I married Jo, and we rubbed along happily enough together. But, oh how we worshipped the material things of life. And we missed them when little junior arrived and we were forced to curtail them. You have seen the advertisement, 'I thought my sheets were white until . . .' Well, thus it was with us. We thought we were happy until you came to live next door to us, and we saw the radiant happiness which shone from your faces and which manifested itself in all your actions. We then knew that you had something which we had not and which we wanted.

"You know what followed. The tentative approaches and the timid withdrawals. What difficult and disappointing months they must have been to you, before you finally succeeded in getting a word across to us, and then, praise God, the day came when you managed to place those great issues before us and we were compelled to face them. I confess, Bob, that I was unable to understand you, and I even resented your approach. Why pick on me? I was not living a bad life. There were plenty of chaps who led a far worse life than I. How I called on science to help me again, as it had in days gone by. But somehow, this time, it could not help me at all, and I became exceedingly miserable.

"There followed that terrific Monday night. Jo came home from the hospital where she had been nursing and told me of a fellow nurse who for no apparent reason, had suddenly commenced to pass on to Jo the same glorious message that we had received from you. The impact of this was tremendous. We could not possibly deny it. And then came the last great fight . . . we struggled gamely on for another couple of hours, producing this hopeless argument and that, as our old values and old lives began to crumble all around us. The end came quite suddenly at midnight. We searched wildly for one more round to fire at the Enemy, and found that the ammunition was exhausted. There was only one thing left to do. SURRENDER! As we surrendered, it was as though the sun rose above the dark and chaotic battleground of my mind. Its rays touched one dark corner after another and showed me what lay hidden there.

"I saw that for years I had worshipped a false god—myself—and that god was rapidly reduced to dust. I saw the tremendous sin of ingratitude I had committed and knew that I was worthy of death. I saw the meaning of that story I had loved as a child; saw in fact that Christ had died for me personally; had taken my great weight of sin with Him in order to secure my reprieve; and had risen again that I might have abundant and everlasting life. I saw, and I rejoiced, and I worshipped. And the wonder of it all was that Jo saw all this with me!

"My dear friends, the story does not end here. Already we have other great chapters to add, and may it please God that there will be even greater ones in the future. But no matter what the future holds, nothing will ever occupy such a warm spot in my heart as that precious moment when Christ succeeded in breaking through to me and showing me such wonderful love, even though I had spent years in perpetuating His crucifixion.

"I pray that it may be in His will that we should all be used by Him to His glory. No matter what we can do or endure in His Name, it will be little enough when compared with what He has done for us. May He give us strength and wisdom to show others the way out of their prison camps. Your brother in Christ for ever. Doug."

Now I wonder what this moving account has meant to you? Naturally to us it brings back treasured memories. Doug and Jo are now much older, but their faith still rests in the One who so gloriously saved them. It was such a joy to meet them again not long ago, and to share happy fellowship together.

Shortly after their conversion, a young student staying with us in our home became very restless, and although a professing Christian for years, said to us . . . "Why haven't I got the joy of those two next door?" When I suggested that she might be witholding something from the Lord, possibly her personal ambition to be a successful teacher, this young woman went to bed in a huff. For some days she actually ran a temperature fighting the Lord. It most unfortunately coincided with her finals at the University, and we were deeply concerned.

However a few days later the most radiant young woman approached us and said, "I have at last surrendered everything to Him, and I cannot express the joy and depth of my new found Christian experience. I can now understand what has happened next door!" Con passed her exams with honours, and after a few years of teaching went out to Alaska with Wycliffe Bible Translators where she still rejoices in doing His will. You see, she had to get where Doug and Jo had started their Christian life, at the point of full surrender.

Last night I heard a professor on a TV programme say, "Being a Christian means doing the will of God." Ah, that's it. When we commit ourselves to Christ and submit to the will of God, then the joy of salvation becomes a reality in our lives. Doug and Jo surrendered. Con surrendered. It's when we come to the end of our little kingdom, that we enter into His. It's when we bow the knee in submission that our conversion, like Paul's, bears the stamp of God in the fervent declaration of our heart as we say, "Lord, what will thou have me to do?"

Will you surrender to Him now? Somewhere along the line you are holding back. You believe the doctrine, but you resist doing His will. Christ said, *"If any man will do His will he shall know of the doctrine."* It's more than experimental. It's an eternal commitment. Yield to Him this moment. Don't hold a single thing back. Let Him have everything. Then, like Doug and Jo, you will see, and rejoice, and worship. *Remember, "Not every one that saith Lord, Lord, shall enter into the kingdom of heaven, but he that doeth the will of my father which is in heaven."*

9   Missionary Memoirs

> *My Word shall not return unto me*
> *void.*   (Isa. 55: 11)

The year is 1940, and Cynthia and I have moved from
Pedapalli in Hyderabad State, and are now situated in
Tadepalligudem, in the Madras Presidency. The
country is flat and beautiful, largely due to the irriga-
tion made possible by the many canals which bring the
waters of the River Godavari for many hundreds of
miles inland. Instead of bare, barren stretches of land,
one is confronted with mile after mile of paddy fields,
the soft green colour being so restful to the eyes.
General Sir Arthur Cotton, the engineer largely responsible for the construction of these canals, was a
family connection of Cynthia's grandmother, an interesting link with the district.

The bungalow we are occupying is very roomy and
airy, close to the village of Prattipadu. Like Pedapalli,
it is also a haunt for snakes and scorpions. The sails
of the barges in the moonlight, with palm trees sil-
houetted against the sky, are delightful.

We are responsible for some forty-five villages along
the banks of the canal, and our first trip by houseboat
is a new experience. Fitted out with two spacious
rooms, folding beds and tables, bathroom and cook's
quarters, it enables us to get out and unhurriedly meet
the people in these areas.

On our first trip we set out with our 'ayah', cook
boy, boatman, and evangelists. On either side and
stretching as far as the eye can see, are beautiful green
paddy fields, dotted here and there with palm trees and

relieved by an occasional clump of vegetation, indicating a village.

We travel slowly, the boat being drawn upstream by coolies, and punted down. Presently, the green fields give place to groves of mangoes or bananas. Bunches of stately coconut palms wave their majestic branches in the breeze, proudly revealing masses of new green nuts. Lazy water-buffalo gaze wearily at us as they bathe contentedly at the water's edge.

We have now been seen, and the word passes that the *tella dora* (the white man) has come. Our children, Peter and Joy, are the object of attention on the bow of the boat. Women and girls with their gleaming brass water-pots and gaily coloured saris, pause to smile shyly. Countless numbers of laughing and chattering children, their brown naked bodies gleaming in the sunshine, crowd alongside to catch a glimpse of our little family, a rare sight indeed. Nearby, oxen tread out the corn which is quickly gathered into sacks by a singing crowd of men. A heavy old ox-cart ambles along the dusty road. Papyia, guava, pomalo, orange, lime and other tropical fruits stick their heads over white-washed compound walls. It is all very delightful, but a mere veneer covering the appalling sinfulness of men.

We drop anchor under some shady cork trees, which shed their delicate white fragrant flowers as a welcome carpet, and the work begins. We spend a few days here, cycling to the surrounding villages as we feel led, and then push on. What an advantage to have such a mobile house free from snakes and scorpions and fit for all weathers. At Mundapaka, we had several meetings with the Christians and the response was good. They were anxious that we should have an open-air Gospel meeting in their *palem,* and we were glad to do so, the Holy Spirit enabling me to speak in Telugu as never before, as I simply gave myself to Him for the sake of those perishing souls around me. It was exhausting, but we all felt that the Lord was doing something very real.

A night or two later, just as we were retiring, I saw two young men standing in the shadows on the river bank. "We have come to see you, sir," they said.

Before I had time to answer, they had seized the rope, drawn the boat to the bank and had scrambled aboard. One of them had an ugly knife with him.

Seeing my questioning look they produced some green coconuts and began to hack the tops off, offering some to me for a drink. I was much relieved. Five years in the east made me realise that something lay behind this peace offering.

Gratefully accepting the delicious refreshment, I began to talk to them about Christ. Their faces lit up, and I recognised one of them as a patient whose cut finger we had been treating, and the light began to dawn

"Do you desire to follow Christ?" I asked.

"We do!", they almost shouted with joy. What a prayer and praise meeting we had; then arousing the evangelists, we stayed up for an hour or two encouraging them in the Word, before they left. They had been convicted and convinced during our open-air meeting.

Navepalem lies three miles further up the canal, and Malachi (one of our part time evangelists) and I, set off to preach the Gospel there. After spending some time in the open air, and distributing a few tracts to those who could read, we saw a number of men squatting on the veranda of a nearby house. They were watching us intently.

We approached with the usual Indian greeting which assured us of a welcome, and immediately they asked us to tell them more about "our religion" which is always a good subject of conversation.

One of the men, an orthodox Hindu, with painted face and tied up hair, seemed to come under deep conviction as he listened to what we had to say. How futile were his religious exercises in the light of such a free salvation, so seemingly impelling and true to every seeker. But it is a costly way.

Trying to find a means of escape from the truth which would justify his orthodox beliefs in the eyes of his relatives, he exclaimed suddenly with a note of triumph in his voice . . . "Have you ever seen Jesus Christ? How can you believe what you say if we cannot see Him?" There were nods of approval and agreement on all sides.

Before I could take up his challenge, a woman's voice was heard from within the house.

"Venkataswami, you have laboured for many years in this place, reaping the benefit of your crops. Have they satisfied your heart? Has your religion brought you peace?"

She spoke words of deep-seated conviction filled with such assurance that it caused him to blaze with anger and for a few moments there was pandemonium. Shouting, abusing and challenging her, he rose to his feet and stormed into the house, scattering a group of women and children, as he squatted down in front of her, continuing his oration more vehemently than ever in a torrent of abuse. Would a mere woman dare give such a reply.

Meanwhile, the other men were also taking up the challenge outside, and were making as much noise as possible!

The woman could not answer many of his learned questions, but her calm attitude and peaceful expression made him more angry than ever, causing us to wonder at the evidence of the new birth being made manifest in her actions.

After the uproar had subsided, we pointed out that God was a Spirit, whose presence and transforming power could be experienced in lives yielded to Him, but like the wind, He could not be seen with human eyes. At times, the Godavari Delta is devastated by hurricane force winds and torrential rains, but had he ever seen those winds? I can picture him now, looking at the waving branches of a palm tree as I spoke, thinking intently. However, he and his friends abruptly left us, making some excuse, and we were left alone with the woman and her husband who asked intelligent questions, a man hungry for reality with a quest for the truth.

How glad we were to have a profitable time with them, quietly discussing the claims of Jesus Christ, the only true and living God.

Then the woman produced a small bag out of which she took a Bible, a hymn book and a book of Bible stories. She must have been in the habit of carrying these around with her as she was now on a visit and had come quite a distance. As we talked together, her countenance shone with the light of heaven. We had discovered a disciple of Christ, not yet baptised, but faithfully witnessing for her Lord alone, amongst her own caste people.

She asked us to pray for her and her husband, and told us how she heard the Gospel at the local hospital when she came as a patient. It was there that she embraced the truth for herself. It seems amazing that this woman had discovered what thousands in our so-called Christian country have never discovered. She had found in a personal relationship with Jesus Christ the answer to her deepest needs. The Lord had become her Saviour and she was rejoicing in the glorious experience of sins forgiven.

Right there, in the midst of all the darkness of Hinduism, the Light was shining through.

In all these wonderful experiences in our missionary adventures, we rejoice in God's goodness. We have been so privileged to see His hand at work in so many marvellous ways, but of course it has not been without its times of testing. Little did we realise that a few weeks after these wonderful times of blessing our little son Peter would be on the point of death with dysentery, that Cynthia would be semi-delirious with typho-malaria, and that at the same time we would bury our darling little daughter, Joy. It's perhaps good in many ways that we do not know these things before they come to pass.

One day in Hyderabad State we visited a village, which had little light of the Gospel and commenced an open-air meeting at a junction of a number of walls. We knew from experience that walls have ears, many coming to listen from the other side without being seen. Paul was giving his testimony. He had found the Lord when on a painting job in the city, over a hundred and fifty miles from his own village. Somebody gave him a tract which he took back with him, and although it gave very little information, a group of people turned away from their idols and began in their own way to worship the living God. Then our predecessor visited their village and preached Christ to them. They immediately recognised Him to be the One whom they were worshipping, and a little church was formed. It was in this village that Jesuratnam, mentioned in a previous chapter, lived.

After Paul's testimony, a young man who had been listening intently said, "I pray to God." Thinking him to be a Hindu expressing his views, Paul asked, "But which God do you worship?"

"Jesus Christ", he replied.

We almost fell over backwards with amazement.

"Where did you learn about Him?", was our next question. Then taking off his *pugree,* the lad stood upright and in faltering tones, with tears in his eyes, he repeated the Lord's prayer in Telugu before the large crowd, which was by this time growing rapidly.

There was a touch of God upon this remarkable event. Here in a heathen village, without the light of Christ, was a young lad confessing the living God before his own people. He had simply learned the Lord's prayer from a Christian worker, hundreds of miles away, when he had gone to work in a large town, and with that Light he had come back to his own village. Was it not the hand of God that guided us to go there when we had almost decided to visit elsewhere that day?

As we were rejoicing over the lost sheep which had been found, the boy's father came on the scene. He was furiously angry when he discovered what had happened, and ordered the boy into the house. Turning to me, the lad said, "Sir, I must go," so telling him where we had come from and committing him to the Lord, we gave him leave.

As soon as he approached his father, the latter gave him a staggering blow across his face, and the last we saw of the young man was him cowering under his father's blows for Jesus' sake. Here was the only light in the village of Ratnapuram, and a caste boy at that. His name was Balayah.

When a number of British officers and servicemen got lost in the area of Pedapalli, and discovered us living there, they couldn't believe it. No shops (apart from the Indian bazaar), no luxuries, cafés, places of amusement or entertainment, amenities, radio, electricity or gas, running water, friends or relatives of the same outlook, European food, hospital, doctor . . . NOTHING as far as they were concerned.

Yet we had everything! We had Christ and He satisfied and sanctified all that we possessed. We did not endure life there . . . we enjoyed it. If He could do that for us, surely He can do much more for you, because He cares.

10   "YFC" or "YFC"?

As many as received Him . . .
(John 1: 12)

New Zealand is a beautiful country and we lived for
a time amongst the farming community in the Waikato
district. Our youngest daughter was born in Morrinsville, and I remember when I was asked to speak at a
"Youth for Christ" meeting in this town. It was adver-
tised as a "YFC" rally, and as usual it attracted quite
a large number of young people. One young lady
thought that the initials "YFC" stood for "Young
Farmers Club" and she came along to see what it was
all about! She was a most unusual young woman—
attractive, vivacious, and a great lover of horses. She
had trained her own beautiful animal to do almost
everything a horse was capable of doing. As a tele-
phonist in the local exchange, her only ambition was
that of owning the most magnificent horse in the neigh-
bourhood, and she was well on the way to success in
this realm. This desire eclipsed everything else, so that
she was not even interested in a boy friend. As far as
Christian things were concerned she was completely
ignorant of God's way of salvation. In fact, she hardly
gave the matter a thought. She came to the Youth
Rally that night thinking it might be a social occasion
for young farmers to get together. She received the
shock of her life to discover it was a Gospel meeting.

I remember speaking on the life of Abraham that
night, how this man had stepped out in faith and trust
to believe God in the midst of heathen darkness, and
how God had dealings with him to bring him to the

place of complete and absolute surrender to His will. I went on to say how God had provided a substitute for our sins in the light of the ram caught in the thicket when Abraham was about to slay his son, and that apart from the Cross of Calvary, where the Lamb slain from the foundation of the world had been slain for us, there was no forgiveness or hope of eternal life. Pauline was listening carefully. She had never heard anything like this in her life. Her home was not a happy one, and she was often very lonely. Perhaps this was why her horse meant so much to her! The Holy Spirit was working in her heart and at the close when I made a short appeal for anyone to come forward to get right with God, two young people responded. One of these was Pauline. It was then we heard the story of why she had come to the rally. She came like Zacchaeus, out of curiosity, only to go away with the Lord Jesus Christ as her own personal Saviour. She went home with a new purpose in her heart, and a new life to live for God. Pauline became a radiant Christian right from the start. It was a wonderful conversion.

The impact made in the community and amongst her own people was fantastic. That something had happened to her was undoubtedly apparent to all. I shall never forget the occasion, several weeks later, when arrangements were made for her public baptism. Many people had gathered from all directions to witness her confession of faith in this way, but it never took place. Relatives turned up and demanded the postponement of the ceremony. Surely she was too young in her new-found faith to know what she was doing! It was obvious that they were not only angry, but bewildered at this turn of events. Some of us felt for their sakes that a postponement might be the wisest move, and it was decided to acquiesce. However, they bargained with us for a month's grace, that if she was of the same mind in four weeks' time we would go ahead with the ordinance. It was obvious that they would do all in their power to get her to change her mind, but we knew that nothing would persuade Pauline to do this. She was simply radiant in her witness for the Lord Jesus Christ.

Four weeks later to the day Pauline turned up to be publicly baptised and there was no stopping her testimony for the Lord. Her Bible found a prominent place at the local telephone exchange and she became an ardent follower of the Master. No one could fail to note that here was a young Christian woman bubbling over with joy that was infectious to a degree. She lost no time in buying up every opportunity for Christ. God had raised her up to be a testimony to the whole community.

As the weeks and months went by, Pauline began to have dealings with God over many things in her life. She began to think in terms of becoming more useful to Him and resigned from the Post Office in order to take up nursing. Then she wanted to visit us, for we had since left for Fiji. We welcomed her warmly, and it was wonderful to see her enthusiasm as she borrowed my piano-accordian and went out into the villages to witness for the Lord.

We were taken aback when she told us quite calmly how her fare had been provided. She had gone to the shipping office and booked everything by faith. When she was asked for the balance of payment, she said quite simply, "Oh don't worry about that. The Lord will provide it in good time!" The young agent was dumbfounded. He replied something like this, "I don't know what it's got to do with the Lord, but we want the money!" This was, no doubt, a further opportunity for Pauline to witness, and she promised him there and then that all would be paid in due course.

The details of how she went to Auckland to a missionary rally instead of spending a holiday weekend with some other young people, have escaped me, but it was when she was leaving this rally that someone known both to my wife and myself met her on the steps of the building outside. This person was almost bowled over. During the missionary meeting her heart had been exercised about helping Pauline and she had said to the Lord, "If I meet her today, I will give her some money," specifying a certain amount. Incidentally, she thought she was fairly safe in making that decision as she imagined Pauline to be many miles away! One of the first people she met on the steps of the building was Pauline, and the money was the equivalent required to pay the balance on her deposit for fares to Fiji!

Pauline completed her nursing training with the object of going to Bible College in Auckland. There was one big problem, her horse. Friends had been caring for this lovely creature on their farm and everyone wondered what might happen if Pauline should be called away to some other country. One day it jumped over the door of its new home to make its escape, but in so doing it caught its head on a beam and died from concussion. Pauline accepted this situation as from the Lord. She was naturally grieved over its death but rejoiced to think that there would be no idol standing in the way of her future plans which were now in the Lord's hands.

After Bible School, Pauline met a fine young man who had emigrated from Holland to New Zealand and whose heart was set in the direction of the mission field. His name was Paul, strange to say, and the happy couple set out for work amongst the Aborigines in Western Australia where they laboured together for some years. They are now back in New Zealand raising a lively little family and as keen as ever to witness for their Master. We have met them in Australia and New Zealand from time to time, and thank the Lord for their united testimony which always gives glory to the Lord who saved them both.

Just to think that a young woman who came to a

61

YFC Rally in Morrinsville, New Zealand, believing it to be a social occasion for young farmers, was gloriously converted and has been used of the Lord in bringing many others to Christ since then! We can never underestimate the value of one precious soul who finds the Saviour, which should be an incentive for us to speak to others and to bring them along to our church meetings from time to time. How I thank God for that Saturday night rally in New Zealand! I'm beginning to wonder what the young people are doing in this country on a Saturday night, as so few seem to be attracted to meetings of this nature. Does your church have an outreach for young people like this?

11   Over the Precipice

Be ready always to give an answer to
every man . . .   (1 Pet. 3: 15)

The picturesque winding hills and mountains of New
Zealand's delightful countryside became even more
enchanting as we approached beautiful Lake Taupo.
We were on a visit to this lovely country after a few
years' absence and had been loaned a car for the purpose of conducting evangelistic meetings by our dear
friend, the late Mr. Robert Laidlaw.

It was a perfect day, and the clear reflections on the
distant lake are quite characteristic to those who know
the area. Framed in mulga bushes and yellow broom,
the shimmering blue water reflects the distant snow-
capped Mount Ruapehu, an active volcano which
betrays itself with its plume of dusty smoke lazily
merging with the majestic clouds which look down on
the beauty beneath with lofty contempt. Here and
there the hills are dotted with jets of steam emerging
from cracks in the ground, and simmering hot water
pools betray these active thermal regions.

We rounded a bend to discover a lay-by for tourists
protected by a stout fence, and pulled into the bay to
get a wonderful view of the area from this look-out on
the edge of a precipice. It was quite breathtaking, and
I found myself taking some coloured photographs of
this magnificent panorama. At such times the words
of a lovely hymn run through my mind and sum up
the situation from the Christian standpoint.

Heaven above is softer blue, Earth around is sweeter
  green,
Something lives in every hue Christless eyes have
  never seen.
Birds with gladder songs o'erflow, flowers with
  deeper beauties shine,
Since I know, as now I know, I am His and He is
  mine.

As we stood surveying the awe-inspiring scene, our silent reverie was interrupted by the raucous sound of an approaching motor-cycle, and before we could realise it the fence nearby was completely shattered as the vehicle disappeared with its rider over the edge of the cliff. He had taken the bend much too quickly with disastrous results!

In a moment our delightful preoccupation was changed to a desperate panic. What had happened? Was there any chance of a rescue? Had the rider been killed? Dashing to the broken part of the fence we saw to our great relief that the motor-cycle, complete with rider, had been miraculously caught in a stout thicket several feet below. It would require some considerable skill to pull him to safety, and in the meantime he dare not move. In any case he seemed to be stunned by the whole situation. It wasn't long before we were joined by others who drew alongside to see if they could help. In next to no time ropes were available which were soon hitched to a truck as someone volunteered to go over the edge to pull the vehicle and its rider to safety.

While this was going on, one of the rescuers was encouraging the young man to take things easy as he was hauled up the bank. It was obvious to him and to all of us that only a miracle had saved him from plunging down the slippery slope into eternity. As soon as the situation had improved and there was no further cause for alarm, this willing helper began to exhort the young man to thank God for his escape and we found him to be an active Christian worker. In fact, we soon recognised him to be a man who wanted to meet us personally, someone who was anxious to contact us during our short stay in New Zealand! He had been wonderfully converted from a profligate life and was now a radiant witness for the Lord. You can imagine the conversation from there on!

There was no need for the young motor cyclist to be preached at from our vantage point. In his precarious position he could not help hearing two Christians rejoicing in their wonderful experience of salvation as he was slowly hauled inch by inch up that precipitous slope. It was now quite laughable! Rescued from death in a miraculous way, he now listens to a heavenly conversation above him as he is dragged slowly up the slope backwards. It must have registered, especially as he was compelled to stare at the edge over which he could have been dashed to pieces.

We had no need to hurry him up, as it was an inch by inch haul to safety. No doubt it was one of those moments in his experience planned by the Lord Who cared for his soul. He heard plenty to convince him that his rescuers were sent by God not only to save him from sudden destruction but to warn him about the Judgment to come! If he had raised his eyes to see the glorious horizon with its magnificent view as we saw it, instead of looking down into the dismal chasm beneath him, he might have been convinced of the truth that there is a Heaven to be gained as well as a Hell to be shunned. Few could have listened to the Gospel at a more appropriate time. It seemed that both his obvious deliverance from death and his sudden confrontation with the Gospel had stunned him into complete silence.

We got him back on the road a very shaky man, and as he wobbled off to the nearest village for repairs to his motor-cycle, his ears were resounding with the

Gospel challenge. Our friend told us that he would follow him up and see if he could be of further help, and we continued on our journey thankful to be of service to someone who had been mercifully spared from sudden destruction.

We often wonder if that man ever responded to the Lord. At least we know that this alarming incident was a link in the chain of events that so often brings a man under conviction of sin and prepares him for the time when he accepts Jesus Christ as his Saviour and Lord. We trust that this has happened in the young man's experience.

God moves in mysterious ways His wonders to perform . . . and oft times accidents of this nature are allowed to bring someone to Christ. Of course, this is not always the case. The fact that two of this young man's rescuers were Christians who had never met until that moment is a very strong argument in favour of God's intervention. It must have struck the young man quite forcibly that there is a living bond between the Lord's people who have never met before, and that they also speak the same language.

Perhaps the most wonderful part of this story lies just there. The timing of the situation was unique. Christians waiting on that deceptive bend and Christians following up behind the young motor cyclist, ready to give a helping hand and witness at the same time! I feel sure that if the Lord's people were in the Spirit and always available in every emergency and contingency, we should constantly be seizing unique opportunities where our testimony would count much in His service. We are called to be witnesses, not necessarily preachers or tract distributors, and much of this witnessing is spontaneous. The world is not impressed by Christians who seek to "button-hole" people into Christian conversations or pressurise people into making decisions. If we are prepared to give a ready answer to the hope that is within us when God's opportunity presents itself, life becomes quite exciting—to others as well as to ourselves.

Apart from the fact that this young man had been saved from certain destruction by the intervening hand of God in preparing a forked branch of a tree to grab the motor cycle on its downward plunge, the conversation above him as he heard two Christians rejoicing in their experience of Christ must have been arresting to say the least. To me this is the greatest miracle of that rescue. Worldly people would have attributed his deliverance to just "luck" and congratulated him on his fortunate escape. It would have ended there. But to hear the Gospel in such a reassuring and positive manner under such circumstances must have made that young man more God-conscious than anything else in his life. It was so remarkable, that I am hoping one day to meet that young man in eternity and hear the rest of the story . . . unless of course, I hear it down here at some time or another.

We have no idea what today will bring forth in the way of an opportunity to be witnesses to our Lord, and when we do meet some fellow Christian on life's pathway, what a joy it is to share fellowship together.

A few days ago I had to deliver a parcel of literature to London Airport for a speedy overseas despatch to Monte Carlo. Imagine my great joy when a radiant Indian Christian, seeing the consignment note made out to Trans World Radio said, "I know these people. They have asked me to make tapes for broadcasts in Urdu"; and we spent the next few minutes sharing our Christian experience. I then found that he had been led to Christ in India by one of my own personal missionary friends! I am sure that others in that office must have sensed the immediate oneness and fellowship between us which is so infectious to an outsider.

Maybe our Lord meant this when he said, *"By this shall all men know that ye are my disciples, when ye have love one for another."* When our spirits witness with His Spirit that we are the children of God, miracles take place. May that be so in our experience today.

12   Borrowed Power

And he put out his hand and took it.
(2 Kgs. 6 : 7)

Have you read the story of the lost axe-head in the
second book of Kings chapter six? It is indeed worth
reading. Apparently the sons of the prophets felt the
spiritual atmosphere somewhat restricting under the
leadership of Elisha. He had already saved them from
death by putting an antidote into the pot of herbs containing a poisonous variety, and one of them, Gehazi,
had been stricken with leprosy because of his covetous-
ness and dishonesty. It was quite obvious that God
was making His presence felt in a very real way.

Some people don't appreciate being hemmed in like
this, and the sons of the prophets were no exception.
Provided they adhered to scriptural principles, and were
sound in doctrine, they were quite happy to be considered a specially chosen few who spent their time
studying the Word of God. It never occurred to them
that God wanted them in the forefront of battle, and
that He would arbitrate over their waywardness and
sinfulness. They no doubt had a formula for all these
things including regular confession and set times of
prayer.

It was a frightening experience to live too close to
the man of God, Elisha. Things were getting a bit
hot. Maybe it would be good to expand. That is why
they suggested building a bigger place, with perhaps
separate rooms for each of them. Elisha consented
to go with them, but as one man was felling a beam,
his axe-head fell into the river Jordan and immedia-

tely his usefulness had gone. Not only that, the axe wasn't his property, which made things ten times worse. He would have to give an account to the owner and his dismay knew no bounds. *"Alas master,"* he cried. *"It was borrowed."* Elisha went with the young man to the scene of the accident and miraculously found the axe-head where it had disappeared, restoring it to the young man who was eternally grateful. Perhaps this was the same young man whose eyes were later opened to see the Lord of Hosts . . . at least his language is the same, for when surrounded by the enemy he used a similar expression, *"Alas master, what shall we do?,"* later feeding his enemies instead of exterminating them, learning something entirely new concerning the Kingdom of God.

This remarkable incident of the lost axe-head in the muddy waters of the river Jordan illustrates a spiritual principle which seems to have been lost in the murky shallows of evangelical truth at a time when God is longing to unleash torrents of blessing to thirsty souls around us. Never has the evangelical church had such golden opportunities of presenting the claims of Christ to a wicked degenerate civilisation, and never has she failed so miserably in her attempts to do so. The prominence given to the simple Gospel challenge by nationwide evangelistic Crusades, the release of world-wide religious publications and long playing records, the latest in projectors, tape-recorders, and visual aids, the extensive use of radio, and frequent visitations by world famous evangelists and Bible teachers . . . all these should have given the Church an impetus to manifest the mighty power of God, yet somehow something terribly vital is missing.

Perhaps there is nothing quite so shallow as evangelical shallowness, and our sluggish testimony is mirrored in the murky waters of inconsistency as our spiritual growth is impeded by the overhanging branches of worldliness, and cluttered by the debris of a false profession. Like the sons of the prophets, we would selfishly settle beneath the shade of our dogma on the attractive banks of our beliefs, as we swing our axes out of sheer dedication and devotion to a false sense of duty.

What is the matter with us all? Where have we failed so miserably to grapple with the dreadful world situation as it tragically stares us in the face?

One of the sons of the prophets, in the midst of all his feverish activity, actually lost his usefulness, and his power for service had gone. How could he continue? Have you ever felt like that? Have you come to the place where you realise that all your sweat and toil and tears for Jesus Christ amount to nothing— NOTHING AT ALL? Have you lost your power with God and with man? Oh, this is the sad condition of thousands of the Lord's people in these dreadfully shallow days, when the implications of the Cross seem to have been left out of our presentation and appropriation of the Gospel. Only a few months ago, a man of God much used amongst young people told me that during a time of spiritual blessing, the keenest Christians were those who confessed to the deadliest sins. The young man in our story reported his loss to his master, who insisted on accompanying him to the place where the axe-head fell into the muddy river, and it was then, when he had showed him the place, that the miracle happened. It was not so much the method of its recovery, as the miracle of full restoration and appropriation; *"And he put out his hand and took it."*

Some years ago a young lady shared a personal problem that had been troubling her. She had been systematically taking notepaper from the office where she worked, and because "they were all doing it" she thought little of the consequence. Coming under conviction of sin, she approached one of those axe-swinging evangelists for his advice. "Don't be so sensitive and silly," was his typical reply. "Just tell the

71

Lord about it, and then forget it." But she couldn't do that. She had a conscience enlightened by the Holy Spirit, and shared the problem with me. I told her to obey the Lord whatever the cost or the consequence, and she did. It wasn't easy to confess to the Secretary of one of England's leading manufacturers, but she was accompanied by her Master to the place where she lost her axe-head and, freely forgiven, she entered into a new lease of life, when the power of the Holy Spirit was restored, and her whole being so transformed that she could never be the same again.

During the Billy Graham Crusade in one of Australia's largest cities, a young woman who responded to the appeal went immediately to the University where she confessed that she had fraudulently obtained her degree. By no means an easy thing to do, but she did it. Her Master went with her to the place of failure, and it was worth everything to get right with the authorities and with God.

Another young man approached a bank official to confess the embezzlement of a small sum of money, fully expecting to lose his job. To his joy and amazement, the official was so moved that he attended the Crusade himself and was gloriously converted. Several months ago a young couple went forward in one of my meetings to have dealings with the Lord, and a few days later were relieved of £1,800, which they handed to the Inland Revenue. Was this price of a released conscience worth it? A thousand times YES, for not only did they enter into blessing, but their own church fellowship, which had been dead for years, experienced a spiritual revival.

Now, before you can get to the place of peace and power in your Christian experience, you may have to return to the place where you lost your axe-head. You may have to pay up some debts, for many Christians are notorious for keeping their creditors waiting. You may have to write a letter of apology, you may have to openly confess to some sin, you may have to say "sorry" to somebody. A few years ago, I had occasion to upbraid my youngest daughter at a family picnic, but felt rebuked in my spirit for the way in which I had corrected her, so I turned to her and said, "Sorry, dear, Daddy didn't mean to say what he said in the way that he said it, although he did mean every word that he said." There was a young teenager with us at the time, and she overheard this remark. Turning to my wife in amazement, she said, "My father has been a leading Christian for years, but I have never heard him say sorry to anybody!"

The shallowness of modern evangelical thought allows for so much inconsistency that it almost condones sin. "TELL THE LORD" is the cry of the hour, and so we fail to realise the need for restitution . . . the need to get right with others before we can really claim fellowship with God. In giving advice to a young man whose sin had caught up with him, by suggesting that he confess the matter to his parents, I received the angry retort, "What has my sin got to do with them? I never confess my sin to anyone but the Lord." The answer was simple. "Suppose you stole a hammer from a local store," I replied. "Would you expect the Lord's forgiveness until you were prepared to return it?" Yes, it is vitally essential that we go back to the place where we lost out, before God's power is restored. *"If we walk in the light as He is in the light, the blood of Jesus Christ His Son cleanseth us from all sin."*

May I close by quoting part of a letter received some time ago from someone in New Zealand who came into tremendous blessing as a result of the restoration of his axe-head. This is how he writes:

"I feel I must write you a few lines to tell you what great things the Lord has done for me . . . praise Him. First of all let me say that the Lord has given me a victory every day, and a joy I haven't known in years.

73

I have spoken at a Deeper Life convention and at other meetings. I know the "Keswick Teaching" but somehow to me there was no experience of what I preached. I had been through revival on the mission field, and saw men and women breaking down under the Spirit's mighty power, but all my confessing and seeking God at home here never seemed to get me anywhere. How gracious of the Lord to bring you to this place, and use His Word to break me down. He showed me the awfulness of my sin in His sight. What a hypocrite I had been! Last Sunday afternoon I wept as I tried to tell my wife of my conviction of sin. As we sang 'Love Divine, all loves excelling' at the evening service, the tears just flowed, and it wasn't until I went forward that a real peace came over my soul. Oh, how my heart had been condemning me. It was a humbling experience, but God gave me strength with tears. Today I can praise the Lord for victory. I know the filling of the Spirit is the birthright of every believer, but for so long He was unable to fill me . . . an unclean vessel."

Dear reader, as we shall all have to give an account one day of every moment we have spent here on earth as Christians; as the time is borrowed, and the power loaned to us, let's be sure of getting back to God, to the restoration of the axe-head at whatever cost. The Master Himself will go with us all the way to the place of failure and sin, as He restores to us the lost axe-head. Remember, *"He put out his hand and took it . . ."* May we be able to do that very thing, to put out our hand and take God's power today.

13 Jennie's Deliverance

*All things work together for good to
them that love God . . .* (Rom. 8: 28)

I was in Western Samoa conducting a Gospel campaign
with much blessing. Many had accepted the Lord
including a sea captain, a huge man, who had been
addicted to drink for many years. Once, when drunk,
he had walked clean off the end of the pier into the
water with an enormous splash at dead of night. It's
a wonder he didn't drown! We were experiencing
great times of rejoicing. The hearty singing of those
dear people will long be remembered, and the delightful setting of those South Sea villages beside the palm-
fringed beaches of coral sand remain in the memory
as vivid pictures. No wonder Robert Louis Stevenson,
who lived nearby for some years, was able to write so
enchantingly his story of *Treasure Island*.

Yet in the midst of all this beauty, with the Lord's
blessing resting upon the meetings night by night,
there was a tragedy taking place several hundred miles
to the south in Fiji where I had left my wife and family
some weeks before. An epidemic of polio had hit the
capital of Suva and subsequently spread throughout
the whole group of islands taking tremendous toll. The
hospitals were overworked and there were quite a
number of deaths as well as the inevitable results of
paralysis. News is always somewhat slow and limited
in the South Seas, and so the full picture of the situation never got through to us in Samoa. We were
blissfully ignorant of what was happening in Fiji, which
was perhaps a good thing in many ways.

The time of my departure arrived and I was garlanded with *leis,* delightful tropical flowers which were heaped upon my shoulders at the wharf and, little realising what lay in front of me, I bade farewell to the Christians with fond memories of a visit which I shall never forget. In a few days' time I would be reunited with my family in Suva, so I anticipated a time of relaxation on board which was most welcome after such an arduous schedule of meetings for six weeks.

As the ship arrived in Suva harbour I was suddenly alerted by a situation which had been carefully shielded from me by my wife and family. I noticed my youngest daughter, Jennie, was not with the family at the wharf. This was most unusual and I actually shouted from the deck as we drew alongside, "Where is Jennie . . .?" It never occurred to me that she was one of the polio victims. I learned afterwards that my friends in Samoa were fully aware of the facts, but they, too, had kept the news from me. There was no point in aggravating a situation which could not be remedied, as there were no planes or boats to take me back to Suva until the scheduled time of my departure.

As we drove back to our home my wife shared the news with me. Yes, our little daughter had contracted the dread disease, and as the hospitals were over-crowded the authorities had agreed to let my wife care for her needs at home. The rest of the family had been inoculated to guard against the spread of the infection. Jennie had lost the use of one of her legs but was quite cheerful otherwise. She was so happy to have her Daddy back home again.

They were anxious days. So many children and even adults went down with the infection and there was no knowing just how it would leave its victims. We had to carry Jennie to the bathroom as she was unable to walk, but will never forget one of the songs she used to sing as she sat up in bed playing with her toys and books. It was a chorus she had learned at Sunday

76

School, which had become her favourite. It ran as follows:

> *Why do you let the troubles of tomorrow*
> *Bring sorrow to your heart and burdens too?*
> *For if the Father's eye is on the sparrow,*
> *Then surely He will care for you . . .*

Believe me, this was a real source of comfort to her parents' hearts at any rate. As we heard her clear ringing tones sounding out this lovely chorus, we wondered about her future. Would she be able to walk again? Would we have a crippled daughter? We must surround this situation with prayer. We would let our friends all over the world know about Jennie, and so a chain of prayer was started which encircled the globe on behalf of our little girl.

The doctor was most kind and considerate and arranged for regular visits by a physiotherapist who was giving her services most gladly to the many victims in the area. It was quite an extensive course and we noticed that Jennie was responding to the treatment. A little fellow over the road who had much the same symptoms was not responding at all, and he became permanently disabled. You can imagine how we felt when Jennie exceeded all human expectations and in answer to the volume of prayer which surrounded her she began to make a rapid recovery. Now, apart from a few occasional neck pains and a very slight, almost unnoticeable limp, we have a fine healthy daughter . . .

What can we say to these things? How can we answer the questions of those whose children did not recover? Some of our dearest friends have an only daughter who is virtually a cripple as a result of contracting polio while in India. Are some of God's children His favourites upon whom He bestows His blessings? Perish the thought! God has no favourites. He is totally impartial in His dealings with us all. How is it, therefore, that some of us are allowed to go through much suffering and affliction whereas others seem to get off scot free . . . ?

It is not easy to answer these questions. If we had not experienced something of the other side of the picture, perhaps we would be completely in the dark. As you know, my wife and I buried two of our little girls one after the other when we were missionaries in India. We will never understand why this was allowed to happen, but we can most assuredly say that the outcome of it has been glorious. The story told in *More Precious Than Gold* has brought more blessing than we can ever imagine. We know of souls who have been gloriously converted as a result of hearing what God can do in bringing His children through the fires of affliction. If through the taking Home of our children, souls can be eternally saved and many hundreds of others blessed, we can actually thank Him for the seeming tragedy which He turned into a triumph. If Jennie could have brought more blessing to others through an incurable polio affliction we would still have given Him the glory. As it is we thank Him for the deliverance. We are told, *"In everything give thanks."*

Maybe some of us have yet to thank Him for something we have been long fighting against: something we have come to regard as a curse and not a blessing, perhaps something we have secretly imagined to be detrimental and not a means of grace. I recently visited the home of an old friend in Devon who is crippled from the waist down with arthritis. Never have I seen a more cheerful Christian woman, using her somewhat painful hands to create the most delightful pictures imaginable. I believe that these oil paintings are all the more beautiful because they contain the element of a victorious spirit which might otherwise have soured her into a most disagreeable old woman, full of self pity. As it is she recently lost her dear Christian husband, a good friend and a most lovable man indeed. Just to think that some of the most painful things such as arthritis and bereavement could ever bring glory to His Name! It was a joy and tonic to my soul to meet Mary again. Who would think that she was operated upon some years ago and is dependent upon only one kidney . . . ?

Such are the reactions to life's problems. The problems themselves often remain unanswered, but it's our reactions to the situations created as a result that really matter, and actually take care of them! How remarkable. That's why the Bible says, *"All things work together for good to them that love God, to them who are the called according to His purpose."* Accidents, human illnesses, disappointments, bereavements, sorrows—all are part of this world's order of things and we cannot blame God for what happens. It is when we take the situation to Him that we begin to see a new picture emerging enabling us to transform tragedies into triumphs.

Maybe the chain of prayer for Jennie's recovery from polio also started a chain of prayer for Jennie's consecration to the Lord? That, of course, is the most wonderful purpose behind the affliction and we would ask you to pray for her that the Lord might take her life and use it to His praise and glory. She is a young married woman now, and has taken up teaching overseas with her husband Trevor, whom she met at a Christian conference weekend in Chester a few years ago. May their lives be dedicated to the Lord as a thank offering for Jennie's wonderful deliverance, when so many others became handicapped or even died as a result.

14 Godavari Lace

Ask, and it shall be given you . . .
(Luke 11: 9)

It had been a tough term for us, and how we enjoyed
the cool refreshing breeze as we relaxed in the fragrant
atmosphere of the Nilgiri Hills in South India! We
were staying at "Monteban", a rest home in
Ootacamund, a place of relaxation for missionaries
and visitors.

My wife, Cynthia, was recuperating from a serious
illness. Our little son, Peter, had recently been snatched
from the jaws of death, and we had just buried our
second little daughter, Joy, less than three years after
Rosemary went "Home".

We had been conscious of the Lord's sustaining
grace throughout it all, but felt it was time we returned
to the UK for a complete change. But the war was on
and there seemed little prospect of this, so we purposed
returning to our sphere of activity in the Godavari
Delta as soon as our health permitted. However, the
Lord had other plans, and we met some missionaries
from the north who invited us to spend some time with
them in New Delhi. From there we might be able to
make satisfactory arrangements to sail to England.
The prospects seemed to be right, and we knew in our
hearts that the Lord had been planning this for us all
along. In due course we took the long railway journey
with Alan and Myrtle to this new sphere of service
for a period of six months.

They were wonderful months. The Christian fellowship in Carol Bagh in the heart of New Delhi was

implemented by meeting many servicemen who were thrilled to find Christian fellowship. Opportunities for ministry in conventions proved to be a real change and were mightily blessed of God. My wife, expecting our fourth little one, benefitted from the cooler weather and we found a busy sphere of opportunity in this new home so graciously shared with us by our dear friends. Many a time the stewpot was filled to the brim on a Sunday as we always expected an unlimited number of Christian servicemen for lunch. One of these men was Derek Thompson, now Secretary of the Manchester City Mission. However, we could not stay indefinitely, so we began to make enquiries about passages to England. It was a crucial stage of the war and only those with priorities would be allowed to leave India. Moreover, our friends were closing their home for the hot summer months and if we did not make reservations on the Hills the situation could prove embarrassing. After praying about the matter we decided to go ahead by faith and book our passages.

There were three big problems. Firstly, the civil authorities had to sanction our departure. I wasn't even known to the committee personally as we had only moved up north just recently. Anyway, we filled in papers and anxiously awaited their reply. A fellow missionary had been cross-examined carefully when he applied, and only under great pressure from the medical authorities was he given permission to leave. Imagine our joy when a letter came back assuring us that, provided the military authorities were satisfied, we would be given the green light to proceed.

This was the next fly in the ointment. I went to Government House for an interview and asked to see the Brigadier in charge. I can still remember his walrus moustache fanning the breeze as he thrust a paper into my hands and abruptly said, "Only if you are dying or mentally deficient can we grant you permission for a passage!"

That was that! I went home and studied the contents. We needed the signatures of two government appointed doctors before we could possibly hope to leave the country. How absurd! Although we had both been ill, and my wife had been at death's door, we now looked the picture of health. The first real winter in the north had actually brought roses to her cheeks. How could we get such a certificate now?

As we jumped into a *jutkah* and made our way to the doctor I almost laughed at the humour of the situation. It would take a miracle to accomplish the desired results. To our utter amazement, the two doctors who examined us were the only medical men we had seen since we arrived in Delhi. One had supervised the only attack of dysentery I had experienced during the whole of my time spent in India, and the other had attended my wife's recent confinement. They knew our case history. I started to take my coat off. "Put it back on, Mr. Stokes," I was told. "We are signing an urgent form for your early departure as we recognise your need to get out of the country as soon as possible! " I was amazed! Another miracle had come to pass.

I returned to the Brigadier, who snorted again, but this time said unbelievingly, "We can do something about the matter now! "

The next problem was that of money. We had nothing. It would cost at least £300 to get home. What could we do about it? It was war time, and folk at home had other things to think about apart from missionary needs. Suddenly I thought of a plan. Godavari lace! As my wife and I walked in the cool of the garden one evening I put the suggestion to her. Some years ago I had been approached by an Indian Christian in the Godavari Delta with the proposition that if ever I found myself in a jam, I could sell at a profit some beautiful lace made by the local people. This was an industry which had grown from a missionary enterprise years before, and I accordingly sent for a sample of lace and began visiting some of the wealthy *memsahibs* nearby. With a borrowed bicycle and a topee on my head I resembled a Chinese salesman, and after a hard day's work I had sold enough lace to feed a canary. It would take years to procure passage money at this rate!

Then I had an inspiration. The US army! They had a buying department in the centre of their barracks. How could I get in with my samples? Well, that's a story in itself, but I managed it and one day found myself talking to the major in charge. He appeared interested and before I realised what was happening a Christian captain had broken in to say, "Why, major, I know this missionary, and whatever he represents I will back him completely!" He was a man who occasionally came to our fellowship meeting, and what a welcome introduction Captain Grasty's proved to be. "Send us as much of this stuff as you can," the major said before I departed.

I wired to Godavari for a supply of lace and before long we were swamped with bundles of this commodity. I don't know how we managed it to this day, but my wife and I sat on the bedroom floor and sorted it all out. We used our own name tags, and made our prices competitive with local supplies. The American authorities couldn't buy enough, and within a matter of weeks our needs for passages were wonderfully met! Then an order came from the US Barracks to stop further shipments. The news had leaked out and Indian merchants began slashing prices until the army found a cheaper source of supply. But our requirements were met, and as far as we were concerned that was all that mattered!

However, there was another big problem! We had been offered shipping berths and had accepted. Then Peter, our son, came down with tropical chicken pox and we knew that if his rash did not clear by a certain date, we would never make the grade. Believe it or not, the very day we were due to report to the shipping authorities, Peter's last spot had disappeared. How wonderful! All was now clear for us to proceed. We left Delhi with thankfulness in our hearts.

When we got to Bombay we found that instead of travelling in segregated communal dormitories, we had been allocated a first class cabin in officers' quarters on a large troopship, and a doctor was there to meet us to ensure that my wife would receive every attention on the voyage! Opportunities for conducting Bible studies with the troops were sanctioned, and peace was declared in Europe when we arrived in the Suez Canal. The Lord had once again met the needs of His servants and proved His great faithfulness. Permission to leave India, priority passages, and the necessary money, had all come to hand in a few short weeks. Even Peter's infection did not delay matters. We learned later that if we had been unable to accept this offer, we would have been compelled to stay in India for another three to four years, as all subsequent shipping was commandeered to bring troops home for some considerable time afterwards.

Have you committed your life to this wonderful Saviour? Do you know the joy of sins forgiven and a life of devotion to His service? If not, you can start today. You can begin on the threshold of a completely new life by confessing your sins, by repenting and receiving the Lord Jesus into your heart right now. Remember, *"As many as received Him, to them gave He power to become the sons of God, even to them that believe on His Name."* Life is an adventure with Christ on board. He wants to bless you now, to reveal His mighty power in you and to answer your prayers. Until you open the door of your heart to His gentle knocking and invite Him into your life, He will never come. Do so today. Do it right now.

15   Esrom's Vision

He that forsaketh not all that he hath,
cannot be my disciple.   (Luke 14: 33)

It was a cold, crisp winter's day in Tasmania. A slight
mist was slowly dispersing in the brilliant rays of the
rising sun. The distant mountains were capped in pink-
tinged snow, as I stood on Wynyard airport watching
the pilot starting up a little Auster plane preparing for
a flight around the district which was to have memor-
able consequences.

My friend, Esrom Morse, a local farmer, was more
than interested in leaving all his earthly possessions
to set up an aerial mission in outback Austrialia. He
wanted to share his burden with me as we circled
around the delightful hills and valleys of his native
land. The plane coughed and spluttered as he swung
the propellor, only to wheeze and gasp with despair
as it sucked in the frosty air. This happened several
times and I wondered at the prospects of a repeat performance a few thousand feet up. "Don't be anxious,
Bob," he smiled. "Once it gets going it doesn't readily
stop! "

We took off over the spectacular peninsula and
headed out to sea to gain altitude before returning
in the direction of those beautiful mountains. Esrom
was full of hope and confidence. He had spent a
number of years amongst the hard drinking crowds
and lonely sheep farmers in outback Australia during
the war, and his heart was greatly moved with compas-
sion towards them. Very little is being done to reach
these people for Christ, and the problem is one of great

distances. With a suitable plane this could be largely solved. He shared his burden with me as we viewed the sun-drenched coastline beneath us. A few minutes later he said, "We are approaching my farm, Bob— I want to sell it and buy a plane for the Lord's work! " I looked below and saw his children waving as he began to circle round. This is a picture that remains a vivid memory, of a man counting the cost of leaving his earthly possessions to serve his Master. I visualised what this would mean, leaving those lovely green lush hills and valleys for the dry and dusty Australian out- back. His wife and family would accompany him. I took a snapshot through the window to remind me of the cost of discipleship as we continued on our journey towards the mountains. The grandeur of such scenery viewed from a tiny plane is totally different to that from a jet air liner, and because I love flying it is all the more wonderful to dangle in space like this. How true it is that *"Something lives in every hue that Christless eyes have never seen"*.

A few years later, Esrom's dream became a reality. Sinking his assets in a modern Cessna he and his family left for Longreach in the far distant outback to set up what is now known as the Outback Aerial Mission. It was, therefore, a peculiar joy for me to be invited to conduct a Gospel campaign at the opening of a newly built chapel in the heart of that needy area, about 1,500 miles from where we lived in Melbourne.

What a contrast to the lush vegetation of his home in Tasmania! Situated in the midst of scrubland, where the saltbush is ideally suited to the rearing of first class Merino sheep and thereby attracts prospectors, Long- reach has a public house at almost every corner of its dusty wide streets. The heat in the summer is almost unbearable. If it did not possess a good airport with regular communications between Townsville and Brisbane, it would indeed be cut off from civilisation in a very real way.

Esrom and his family came to live in this somewhat outlandish place for the sake of the Lord. It was a joy to be able to help them for a short time in their wonderful witness for Christ. We had some exciting meetings with quite a number accepting Christ as their Saviour, including a few outstanding conversations. I was struck by what a prominent businessman had to say when I started to talk to him on spiritual matters. Cutting me short, he interjected, "Mr. Stokes, if I want to talk about these things I will go to Esrom Morse. He is the one man in whom I have complete confidence! " What a wonderful testimony! Could the same be said about you or me in our own locality?

I learned quite a few things when I was there. Many of the neighbouring farms are hundreds of miles apart and only receive a visit once a year from a minister of religion who calls to receive a subscription for the church! Esrom, who flies to these places, visiting schools and conducting meetings, flatly refuses to accept financial help from anyone who is not a committed Christian, and this has literally amazed them. To think he has sold his farm to purchase a plane with the object of helping them, and won't even accept any money is incredible!

Consequently he has an open door for many hundreds of miles, and his parish extends as far as his plane will take him and his equipment. He was later joined by another dedicated worker in whose home I have stayed, but I must tell of an experience I had when I accompanied him on one of his missions.

Was it not more than interesting to discover that the local evangelical Presbyterian minister was also a qualified pilot, who was overjoyed when Esrom turned up with his plane? It thrilled me to think that, as the work progressed at the new Gospel Chapel, this man joined in to help the boys make model planes! Esrom and his friend took me on an expedition in the Cessna which will never be forgotten in more ways than one.

We were to visit a remote farmhouse quite a distance away. I sat behind the two men to discover that they delighted to make the most of the journey by skimming low over waterholes in search of kangaroos and other wild animals. When we climbed to a good height I was amazed at the barrenness of the countryside, relieved here and there by a remote farmstead. At last we came to our destination and I looked for the runway which is quite a common sight at the sheep ranches. There was nothing to be seen but a rough cart track. I learned later that Esrom is one of the few pilots who lands his plane in areas like this; so after circling around for a few minutes, which was a sign to put the "billy" on down below, and also to give Esrom a good idea of the suitability of his target area, we bumped along the track to pull up outside the farm gate in a cloud of dust!

The welcome was as warm as the weather, and I could see how much the folk appreciated his visit. Such a farm may handle a few thousand sheep grazing in hundreds of square miles of scrubland. On the way back we called in at another farm to advertise my meetings, and I learned what a tremendous contribution a plane could make to missionary work in such remote areas.

It was with a wonderful sense of well-being that I opened my silly mouth on the way back and asked Esrom how his plane worked! "Well, its like this, Bob," he said as he pulled on the joystick. My stomach heaved. We dived and rolled and seemed to do everything but loop until I cried, "Stop it, Esrom—I just can't take any more." How the two of them laughed at my helplessness, but believe me, it was almost twenty-four hours before I got over the dreadful sensation of air sickness. Our daughter, Ruth, has often been taken on such expeditions in Melbourne and simply delights in these stunts. She is the only member of the family who has actually looped the loop and loves it!

My friend, if you were called upon to leave your home, your friends and all that makes life so meaningful in lovely surroundings like Esrom's farm in Tasmania, for a hot dusty environment among hard-hearted people for Christ's sake, what would your reaction be? Maybe you have faced up to this challenge at some time or another and deep down in your heart of hearts you have said, "No, Lord." If you visited Esrom's home in Longreach today, you wouldn't sense any regret, because his heart is set on doing the Lord's will.

His farm would be a drag on him today, because he is sowing and reaping another kind of harvest which the Lord is blessing in wonderful ways. He has been tested and tried many times both spiritually and materially, but the Lord has made up to him and his family abundantly. When God is on the Throne of the heart, any environment becomes a Heaven-sent opportunity of witnessing for Christ. We have proved this ourselves. And when the Presbyterian minister's little daughter was found drowned in a corner of the local swimming bath, you can well imagine what a source of comfort Esrom and his wife were to the sorrowing parents. It was another opportunity of witnessing for Christ in that hard-hearted area, and believe me, Christian witness at such times of apparent tragedy is a wonderful thing. These parents were mightily upheld and Christ was glorified. They, too, left all to follow the Master and this was part of the price. I knew and loved that little girlie who was the joy of her parents' hearts.

Yes, our Lord's words are true, *"He that forsaketh not* ALL *that he hath, cannot be my disciple."* Maybe this is His Word for someone reading this now.

16   Can God Provide?

Before they call, I will answer.
(Isa. 65: 24)

We were living in Melbourne, Australia, and I had
just broken my ankle in seeking to obtain a beautiful
wild flower for my wife! We had been driving through
the delightful Victorian countryside when we saw these
lovely blossoms. Leaping from the car on to a bank,
I failed to notice it was full of irregular ditches covered with tall grass, and the next moment I was in
considerable pain. Fortunately Cynthia was able to
drive me home while I clutched the flowers!

We were also busy preparing for the Gold Coast
Crusade and I was worried about the condition of our
car, which indicated mechanical trouble. A young
Christian farmer had recently promised us a gift of
£100 towards its reconditioning or a suitable trade-in,
whichever we felt was best. We had gratefully accepted
this offer as from the Lord, and told him that when it
was needed we would let him know. We were much
moved to think that his own car was in greater need
of repair than ours! It was his deepest concern that
God's servant should remain mobile in the Lord's
service.

So, hobbling about with broken ankle, worried about
the prospects of taking a trailer over 1,200 miles to
Queensland, and busy in the work of the Lord, I was
suddenly confronted one night by a friend who called
to visit us. Seeing our car in the driveway he remarked,
"It's about time you got rid of it Bob." That was just
about enough. I knew it was true all right, but what

90

could I do? I replied, "Morris, I just couldn't face up to the prospect of looking for a car just now. The very thought of confronting dealers with the pressure of work on hand, and incapacitated as I am, would drive me up the wall." He smiled. "Well," he continued, "You ought to get rid of it before you go up north as the new model will be out before you return and you will lose much more on it otherwise." It was good sound advice, and I slept on it too.

Early next morning, however, I had the strange conviction that I should phone up a Christian car agent to make enquiries. Asking him if he had a vehicle which he could exchange with mine together with the £100 that was available, he laughed. "I have a suitable car for you," he replied. "But I would want £400 besides yours."

It seemed hopeless. However, he asked me to drop in with my car for him to reassess its value, saying as he did so that he would be pleased for me to take the car on offer for use during the day. That was very kind of him, and it would help me considerably.

As I drove the car through the busy streets of Melbourne, I was tremendously impressed. I also found that his offer was considerably better than any other dealer's . . . but £400? Where could I find that sum of money? The vehicle would be just right for our work. Why not trust the Lord for it? I showed it to a friend who thought it was a wonderful deal if it could go through. My wife, who had come with me for x-rays at the local hospital, was tremendously enthused. Yes, it would be a marvellous investment for our work and ministry. I made the best use of it that day, and planned to drop my wife off at home, before returning to the garage to pick up our old car.

Can you imagine my surprise when Cynthia came running back to the car saying, "It's ours, Bob. The Lord has sent in the exact amount. There's a cheque in the mail-box earmarked for a car, and it's exactly

£300 . . . Just what we need with the other promise of £100! " We simply stood there and praised the Lord.

When I returned to the garage and casually said that we would make the deal, it was someone else's turn to raise his eyebrows. "You can keep our old car, Alan," I said. "The Lord has given us this one instead." So again we were able to share His faithfulness, and rejoice together in this remarkable provision of a car. The car offered to me that morning was now ours for His service, and without consulting dealers or being frustrated by looking at different available models, the need was met.

But how was all this possible? Who sent the cheque? Did anyone know we needed that exact amount?

The answer can only be attributed to the Lord Himself, as you will now read. The sender of the cheque lived in Sydney, and the amount of £300 was mailed before I even knew that it would be required. It was only that morning I was aware of the fact that the car was available at the price! My friend had posted it completely unaware of the situation, and the best thing was to give him a telephone call, and ask him what prompted him to send this amount.

First let me explain that I rarely heard from this man. It was true that he was aware of the fact that we were having trouble with the old car, but so were many other people besides. How did he know what to send?

When I phoned him and shared the whole story, I could hear him gasp with astonishment at the other end. He said, "Bob, I'm simply trembling all over. It is true that I had no idea what you required, but the Lord made it quite clear to me that I was to send you £300 for this purpose. I'm thrilling all over with sheer joy! " The man was blessed in his soul indeed. Yes, *"Before they call I will answer."* It is another wonderful story of the Lord's great faithfulness, and especially for this man, as it was the very first time he had experienced the timing of God in this wise. You will appreciate this in the light of the next story.

Many years ago, when my wife and I were preparing to leave the Fiji Islands for furlough, my wife casually asked me one day whether we needed much to complete our passage money home to England. Our boxes were packed and lining the passage of our home, and we had already made reservations for the journey with the shipping company. I looked into my diary, and said, "We need exactly £200."

That day, when I was shopping in Suva, I learned that the manager of a bank which had recently opened up, wanted to see me. He was new to the place, and as I introduced myself, he said, "You are Mr. Bob Stokes the missionary?" "Yes, that's me," I replied. "Well," he continued, "I have received the sum of £200 from someone in Austrialia in your name. What shall I do with it?" "Kindly credit it to my account with the bank down the road," I said, and made for the nearest telephone box. When Cynthia came to the phone, I said, "Didn't I say that we needed another £200 this morning for passages?" "Yes," she replied. "Well, the exact sum has arrived from Australia," I told her, and we just praised Him again for His faithfulness. Surely, *"Before they call I will answer."*

It was some time before we discovered the source of this supply. The money had been cabled to us, and no correspondence followed. We did not even recollect the name of the donor, but discovered in our files some correspondence from her dated years before while we were passing through Australia on our way to Fiji. We had only spent a few weeks in the country and hardly knew anybody there. A letter indicated it could have come from a Christian woman by the same name who attended one of my meetings. I accordingly wrote by faith and thanked her in the Name of the Lord. We still did not receive a reply, and as we embarked on our trip home I even wondered if I had inadvertently appropriated money intended for someone else!

Several years passed by before we were again in Australia, and on one occasion my wife was suffering from a migraine attack when we visited a Christian orphanage. As she was quietly resting, a woman turned up wishing to see her. It was none other than the kind giver of the £200 some years ago. How did she know we needed that exact sum? She didn't! The Lord had blessed her through my ministry, and later convicted her on the issue of tithing. She knew she needed to give back to the Lord what she had been witholding from Him, and when she asked how much, the Lord quietly whispered, "Two hundred pounds". When she asked Him what she should do with it, the Lord laid us on her heart and she immediately cabled the amount to a bank in Suva, not knowing our address or our need. It was just like that!

These stories are wonderful enough in themselves, but there is still something I haven't yet divulged. You see, the man who sent in the £300 towards our car had often been envious of his wife who had experienced the Lord's hand in giving in this way, and he longed to enter into a similar experience. Well the astounding thing is that his wife was the woman who sent us the £200 several years before! How amazing that both of them should be involved with the same missionary couple in almost the same way without knowing anything of the specific needs at the time! And to make it all the more thrilling, we believe these are about the only gifts received from them over the years. No doubt they could tell similar stories involving other of the Lord's servants whose requirements have been similarly met.

May this account of His faithfulness bless you and encourage your faith in Him today.

17 The Chinese Dwarf

He that loseth his life for my sake
shall find it.   (Matt. 10: 39)

Hong Kong is certainly one of the most fascinating
places in the Far East. With four million people living
in an area of twelve square miles, it is a skyscraper
city of immense proportions, and its natural harbour
situated in the midst of towering mountains, makes it
most attractive.

During a visit to this delightful part of the world
we were able to meet a number of keen Christian
leaders and share in their fellowship, conducting a
number of meetings and representing the work of
Trans World Radio at the same time. Our visit included
a trip to the Communist Chinese border, an invitation
to a Chinese wedding, and of course the usual shopping
activities, where we were able to obtain some useful
equipment for our ministry at a fraction of the cost
elsewhere.

What amazed us was the stability of the economy
in spite of the Government's housing problem with its
thousands of refugees from Communist China. We
were told that the way in which the British handled
the last political crisis had raised their reputation
enormously, and we saw no signs of disquiet during
the time of our visit.

We stayed with Dr & Mrs Jenkins, of the Haven of
Hope Tuberculosis Sanitorium, in their delightfully
situated home overlooking Junk Bay. Dr Jenkins does
a magnificent job, and his wife is on the staff at the
Baptist College where she has been encouraged to see

many young Asians from a number of countries responding to the Gospel challenge.

One day as I was driven home in the doctor's car, he told me the following story which I thought I would share with you now. It concerns a little Chinese girl who was an orphan and who was brought up by some missionaries. She gave her heart to Christ while she was still quite young, and here it is exactly as the doctor related it.

"The sad thing about this little girl from the physical point of view is that she was very small. She was in fact a dwarf, but by no means mentally retarded. Indeed she had a very good brain, and having been brought up to love the Lord and to love people, she wanted to do as much as she could for others, so she decided that when she had finished school she would train as a nurse.

"Unfortunately, she is considerably less than five feet tall and the result was that when she applied to the nursing school, having passed all the examinations that were necessary for becoming a nurse, she was turned down on the grounds that it would be impossible for her to handle patients in bed, for she could only just see over the top of the bed (that's a little bit of an exaggeration, but not much!).

"This was a great disappointment to her, but she took it in good part and said, 'Well, if I can't go to the one hospital of my choice I'll go to another.' She applied to every hospital in turn that would accept nursing students in the hope that she might become a nurse, but every one of them turned her down. With great disappointment she began to look out for something else she could do, and she was told that perhaps she could be a teacher. She therefore applied to various teachers' colleges here in Hong Kong, but they turned her down too. Again, she was very sad about this, but it's quite understandable that it's much more difficult for a tiny person to keep discipline in a form where many of the pupils may be bigger than the teacher.

"Then someone told her of our place and suggested that since we accepted people of a lower educational standard than the big teaching hospitals, perhaps we would take people with a lower physical standard. And so she applied to us to train as a nurse. Well, it wasn't possible! We had to turn her down for exactly the same reasons as the other hospitals had done. She wasn't big enough to handle a patient who was helpless in bed, and very sadly we told her that we could not offer her a vacancy in our training school. This hit her very hard, but she said, 'Isn't there something else that I can do in order to serve the Lord in a medical or paramedical capacity?'

"We thought quite a lot about it, and then the idea came to us that although she was so small, she could perfectly well sit on top of a tall stool looking down a microscope or doing biochemical tests, and so we offered her a position as a lab technician. Well, it wasn't what she had wanted, but she saw that it was an opening and therefore accepted it. She did the full course of training and grew to like the job . . . to love it in fact . . . and she has become a really first rate little technician capable of doing any of the ordinary routine work which a lab technician has to do day by day. She works over at the clinic where she is the sole technician, and we can trust her to do anything. She really does make a tremendous contribution to the efficiency and also to the spiritual life of the clinic. She has been with us now for I think nearly seven years . . . "

I thanked Dr Jenkins for telling me this story, and as I thought about it I was struck by one outstanding feature—namely that the little girl in question, after giving her heart to the Lord, wanted to do as much for *others* as she could.

She was an orphan. She could have had a big chip on her shoulder. She knew nothing of the love her mother could have given her, and the fact that she was also a dwarf could have led to serious insecurity problems. How wonderful to think that she had learned about the Lord through the kind missionaries who cared for her, and as a result had given her heart to Him.

One day I was passing the clinic and could see this young woman through the window, cheerfully going about her duties because Christ had put His love into her heart. It is just another miracle of His grace. What a difference from the self-centredness of so many in our own country today!

A little Chinese girl, brought up in an orphanage, handicapped by her physical deformity, finds the Lord Jesus Christ as her Saviour and wants to do as much for others as she can! Possessing nothing, and yet having all things her heart could desire in her love for others, she has found the secret of life.

Contrast this with three maiden ladies, living in the lap of luxury, worried about investing another £30,000 to get the maximum returns for themselves! The Christian solicitor who was called in to investigate, told me that he felt like telling them to give it all to others in the service of Christ, as they already had more than enough to keep them in comfort for the rest of their days! The sad part was that they claimed to be evangelical believers!

Our hearts went out to the Chinese Christians in Hong Kong, many of whom are suffering from the affluence of the society in which they live, but others, like this little dwarf, are dedicated radiant witnesses.

I wonder if you have lost the real meaning and purpose of life? You know, it is possible to stagnate as old age aproaches, whether you are rich or poor. It is also possible to make a few enquiries in your neighbour-hood and find out someone who is lonely or sick without home comforts. You have no idea what joy it would bring to your own heart to light that oven and bake a delicious pie which you could take with your own hands to that overworked housewife or lonely old man down the street. There is plenty to do in His Name without visiting psychiatrists to find out what's wrong with an empty, meaningless, existence.

You can see, nothing could be more devastating than to spend your time eating and sleeping, dusting and polishing, shopping and gossiping while you wait for death to remove you from the familiar scene. I shudder to think of it! Remember again what Dr Jenkins said about this little Chinese girl. After giving her heart to the Lord, she wanted to do as much for *others* as she possibly could. It was some time before she discovered God's will, but now she has grown to love the work of a lab technician in serving her Master with a full heart.

Remember, *"He that loveth his life shall lose it, but he that loseth his life for My sake shall find it."*

18   Wally the Bushman

*By the foolishness of preaching to save
them that believe . . .*   (I Cor. 1: 21)

My first introduction to Wally took place in the town
of Bundaberg in Queensland where I was conducting
a Gospel campaign. It was brought to my notice that
a somewhat uncouth young man was in the local
hospital receiving treatment as a result of an accident,
and although the physical injuries were rapidly improv-
ing, there was a general deterioration in his health
which was mystifying the medical authorities. He had
asked to see me because he had heard I was a personal
friend of Billy, Graham. Before I called on him I
decided to find out a few particulars, and I learned
something about his background which was most
interesting.

It appears that Wally had had a most unfortunate
upbringing. Adopted as a baby, he grew up in an
atmosphere of sheer neglect and indifference. His foster
parents seemed to take it out on him, so that at a very
early age he decided to run away, and fend for himself. His education was sadly neglected and he went
"outback" to befriend the Aborigines and to take up
the job of herding cattle from place to place, often
hundreds of miles at a time. The nomadic life appealed
to him. For most of the year he lived under the stars,
often utilising the bare backs of the cattle as his mattress. His frypan frequently contained lizards, witchety-
grubs and even snakes. Tea from a "billy can" heated
on eucalyptus twigs was nectar to his palate. The very
rugged nature of his environment entered into his soul

and his outback existence made him rough and uncouth in his demeanour. He preferred the bush to the towns, the company of wild animals to that of man, and it was merciful that he did not degenerate into the moral abyss of so many who "go native" in this way. So far as I could ascertain he could neither read nor write properly.

Then in a very wonderful way he heard the Gospel. The modern marvel of a transistor radio brought him the good news. Resting under the shade of a coolibah tree one day he heard Billy Graham preaching from Brisbane, and his whole heart responded to the Lord. He had never known anything about God before. Even religion was a mystery to him. Many a time he had passed a church to see people walking in and out and occasionally he heard some hymn singing and wished he could have joined them in his "hill-billies". But he had no idea what it was all about. He often wanted to pop inside and see for himself, but he could not leave the cattle. Totally ignorant of the things of God, he was gloriously converted when he heard over the air the good news that Jesus Christ had come into this world to save sinners such as he. It seemed as though the very works of nature had prepared him for salvation. He knew that somewhere along the line there must be a Supreme Being, but he never gave the matter much more thought. Now he knew. He must see this preacher. He must go at once to Brisbane and meet Billy Graham.

And so like the wise men setting out on their quest to find the Saviour, Wally left his cattle to seek out the Evangelist in the big city hundreds of miles away. When he got there he asked where he could find Billy Graham. Little did he realise that the message he had heard was most likely an "Hour of Decision" programe from one of the local radio stations. Billy Graham had visited Brisbane in 1959, but had left long since. Sadly disappointed, he retraced his steps back into the vast bushland and prayed that someone would be able to help him. It was then that he contacted some Christians in the Bundaberg area and was soon enjoying their company. It was not easy for him, or for them, to try to fit into a new environment after being isolated so long but after a while he got accustomed to the situation and was invited to a youth camp at Pialba nearby. It was at this camp that he met a lovely Christian girl and in his somewhat raw way tried to befriend her. It seemed after a while that his life was now complete. His soul was saved; he was enjoying the fellowship of Christians, and he had found a wonderful friendship with Barbara. She was a very nice girl who tried to help Wally as much as was possible and who grew to love and respect him for what he was.

Then some wise bodies started talking. Barbara was advised for her own sake not to continue the friendship. She would surely regret something that might lead to marriage with such a raw fellow. Eventually she took their advice and somewhat sadly wrote to Wally explaining her decision, not realising what it was going to do to him. She decided to give him up, and her letter came as a great shock. Wally was literally stunned. The only girl he had ever known, the one person who seemed to radiate Heaven to him, had now gone out of his life. He mounted one of his wildest horses and was deliberately thrown from the saddle. But for his magnificent physique, he could have been killed. Mercifully he was found and taken to the hospital in Bundaberg where he was waiting to see me. The only thing that he did not know was that I was acquainted with some of these circumstances which he had carefully hidden from the medical authorities. In fact, he had wrongly invented the story of his accident to cover up the details. Although slowly recovering from the injuries he was rapidly deteriorating in health. In fact, he was a very sick man and a puzzle to the doctors and nurses as he had no will to live.

Wally was most surprised when I suggested that his illness was not due primarily to the fall, but to his disappointment. In fact, it was I who guessed he had deliberately been thrown and I was right. There was no need for him to stay in that hospital a single day longer. If he confessed his sin of desperation and despair to the Lord, and followed this up by another confession to the medical authorities, he could be out of that place the same day. I am sure it was the Lord who gave me such discernment. The authorities knew that as a visiting evangelist I had been requested to call on him, and you can imagine their raised eyebrows when a few hours later, with packed bags, Wally reported that he was leaving. He told them the reason too, and they were much relieved and greatly impressed.

I believe that many physical maladies, not all of them of course, are due to spiritual problems. When a sick person gets right with God, miracles often take place. That doesn't mean we should throw all our medicines out of the cupboard and necessarily resort to "faith healing" but there are times when the Lord can heal without recourse to medicine. I tell you, Wally's testimony must have rocked Bundaberg during those days of special meetings in the new City Hall. News travels fast "outback", and it was a joy to see him coming to the meetings where he saw others responding to the challenge of the Gospel. Later he came to stay for a day or two with my host and hostess, so I was able to get a first hand glimpse of a life that had been shut away from civilisation for so long.

I did a very naughty thing. There were some bushes in the garden resplendent with hot green chillies. I found that Wally had never sampled one before, so plucking one and pretending to eat it, I watched Wally do the same! His reaction was just like a bucking bronco! I laughed and laughed. "Brother", he said, wiping his smarting eyes, "If I wasn't converted, you would be a dead man by now!"

For some time we have lost touch with Wally. Some said that although he got over the broken friendship, he became rather suspicious of certain Christians who seemed to look down on his roughshod ways, and he wandered back into the bush, back to his nomadic way of life. We trust that this time the Word of God has a rightful place in Wally's experience and that he has become a witness to the Aborigines and stockmen in outback Australia, which is one of the world's neediest mission fields.

I wonder if you, like Wally, are holding a grievance in your heart by secretly pining over some great distress or disappointment. This can affect the whole of your spiritual and physical life. Confess the entire situation to the Lord and ask Him for His cleansing and power. Remember, *"If we confess our sins He is faithful and just to forgive us our sins and to cleanse us from all unrighteousness."* When the elders of the early church prayed over a sick man they were told that the prayer of faith would raise him up, but it was added *"And if he have committed sins they shall be forgiven him."* Do you have anything to confess today?

19 The Living Mattress

Be kind one to another . . . (Eph. 4: 32)

Some years ago I learned a great lesson in human kindness! Come to think of it, this rare quality of life, although not mentioned as one of the gifts of the Spirit, is an attribute of God Himself, and the Scriptures often declare this in terms of His loving-kindness. In fact, we are told that love is kind, and we are to "put on kindness", adding godliness and charity. Don't you think a whole volume is contained in the simple phrase, "He's a kind person . . . "! It's a lovely word and a kind individual is usually a delightful person too. I think that children know more of its meaning than anyone else, for to them unkindness is anathema!

We can show kindness in so many ways. A visit to some lonely shut-in with a fragrant pot plant; a thoughtful birthday card to the little fellow next door; a cheery smile and a word of encouragement to the dustman; an offer to do some shopping on a blustery day for the old woman down the street; refusing to listen to some ugly gossip by lovingly changing the conversation . . . yes, there are hundreds of ways today in which we can be kind, perhaps to someone who has been unkind to us! I remember how one of our friends in Australia always gave thanks for his food by acknowledging the Lord's kindness. It was an impression that has never left me. If my wife heard any of our children getting cross or angry with each other she would always say, "Children, be kind to each other! " Its a lovely word. It has a tremendous impact upon any situation.

I was travelling through Malaysia on my way back to Australia from Europe. My wife and I had stayed with missionary friends in Kuala Lumpur, after which she had to fly back to Melbourne to speak at a women's convention. I stayed on for a few days to take further meetings and eventually arrived in Singapore, where arrangements had been made for me to stay with friends, and I found that I was to be entertained by a dear Chinese brother who was more than delighted to have me as his guest. His joy in driving me to his home after work was one of those delights afforded to the Lord's servants in the ministry.

I found that his home on the outskirts of the city was a very clean dwelling and that I would be entertained by him and his son, because his wife and other members of his family had left him when he became a Christian, the price paid by so many of the Lord's faithful servants in other lands. In next to no time he ushered me into a neat little bedroom which was to be my quarters for the next few days, but to my dismay I saw no mosquito netting around the bed. "Oh Lord," I prayed, "Please control these dive-bombers who delight to sample fresh blood whenever I'm around. I'll be useless if I get no sleep!" My prayer was backed with years of experience in India and Fiji, and was wonderfully answered as you will hear later.

Then my host and his son went to the bedroom cupboard and produced some bedding which they carefully spread, in typical Chinese fashion, over a wooden board, which in turn had been placed over a stuffed mattress. It is usual to reverse the process for European comfort later . . . ! Smiling courteously, they bade me goodnight and I was left to it. I noticed, however, that they had deposited a large fly-spray full of insecticide just inside the door, and how I later thanked the Lord for this! Goodbye to all the dive-bombers now! As I turned back to the bed with the fly-spray in my hand, I noticed something quite ominous to those who live in the tropics. I spotted one or two creepy-crawlies on the bedsheet. It did not take long to calculate that if a few could show up in half a minute, two or three hundred could emerge before the night was out. I was right! The humid atmosphere quickly breeds such unwelcome visitors, and the dark cupboard had proved to be an efficient incubator.

As I examined the mattress carefully, I found a family of bed-bugs under almost every button on both sides, with others concealed beneath the beading around the edges. What a gory time I had with my thumb and fly-spray! Hundreds of these creatures were despatched with vigour and lay in heaps on the floor until I could not find a single one left. Then I discovered others crawling out of the joints in the wooden board, and they too were mercilessly swilled to death in the deadly liquid. It took about forty-five minutes to squeeze, stamp and exterminate the enemy, but it was well worth it. Just imagine waking up to find swarms of them all intent on having supper at the same time! I shudder to think of it. However, if there had been a mosquito-net, there might never have been a fly-spray! My friends left this to deal with the dive-bombers, not the ground battalion, and it was indeed a real answer to my prayers. All were under control in a very real way. I had a wonderful night's sleep and I think I only observed one lonely little fellow during the whole of the time I stayed in that home, and he swiftly joined his companions in the dustbin.

Now where does the lesson in human kindness come into this? Well, I will tell you. You see these dear folk had done everything to make my stay comfortable. They gave me the best of their hospitality in every way, and it was not their fault that my unwelcome bed-companions had bred so rapidly. It was certainly not due to uncleanness, as might be indicated in a temperate climate. Vermin just live and thrive in the tropics!

Would it, therefore, be kindness on my part to suggest the next morning that perhaps it might be better for me to look up some of my missionary friends and find accommodation with them? There would be plenty of excuses—no mosquito nets; unaccustomed to Chinese food; valuable contacts in the work; missionary connections in the past . . . yes, hundreds of plausible excuses to change my surroundings, but would it be kind? Would it have shown the love of Christ to my Chinese brother who expressed such delight in entertaining me . . . ? I could have even casually referred to the previous night's experience of the massacre of the innocents by inferring that I was not accustomed to such a performance. No! Better to say nothing—much kinder, in fact, and to this day my friend knows nothing of the dreadful slaughter in his guest's bedroom. Of course, had the Lord not made provision in the wonderful supply of the insecticide, my measles-like appearance the next morning would have given me away! It was a simple case of applying His Word, *"In everything give thanks"* in other words, "Thank you, Lord, for the fly-spray."

I had a wonderful time in that home. I ate Chinese food until I looked like it and even liked it! My friend took me out to enjoy the famous Singapore "steamboat", and I actually relished shark-fin soup, to say nothing of the fact that the fins lie around in the dusty road drying in the sun with stray dogs sniffing at them. It's cooked anyway . . . ! My stay was an experience indeed. I was treated like a king and needless to say my ministry proved to be a real blessing to hundreds of young people. I had no more trouble at nights and slept with a contented heart and a peaceful mind.

What could I do to return my Chinese brother's kindness? In the course of conversation I learned that he very much wanted to get a copy of George Müller's biography. This gave me an idea. Would I find one in Singapore? The evangelical bookshop was changing headquarters so it would be most unlikely that a copy would be available at such short notice. After visiting one or two places, to my amazement I found the only copy available, and it was waiting just for me!

Can you imagine my dear Christian brother's face when I handed it to him before my departure. It was worth the amazed look of intense gratitude, the creased smile and flashing teeth as he unbelievingly took hold of the precious manuscript. To him it was worth more than a million pounds, because it was not only a fulfilment of his desire but also a token from someone who had loved his hospitality in the name of Christ! And if he should find out from reading this book what had happened, I can guarantee his reaction. He would just throw his head back and laugh! You see it doesn't matter any more now. His kindness has not been thrown back in his face. It has been accepted and acknowledged with thanksgiving, and bugs or no bugs it was well worth it all!

20 Joy Through Suffering

It was for the joy that was set before him . . .   (Heb. 12: 2)

What a seeming contradiction in terminology! "Joy, through suffering", yet we read, *"It was for the* JOY *that was set before Him that He endured the cross."*

Someone has said that there was never a moment in our Lord's earthly experience when His life was devoid of joy. His birth was heralded with joy. It was the joy of doing the Father's will that filled His heart at all times. Joy is indeed a very wonderful quality of life unknown to the sons of men apart from redemption. The world knows nothing of joy.

We are living in days when even Gospel preachers suggest that if people want to be happy they should *"come to Jesus"*. Nonsense! People can be happy on their way to hell. Happiness depends on what happens, and has nothing in common with joy. This moral quality of life comes from above, and has been dispensed by the only One who makes joy possible. That is why the early Christians were burned at the stake with the joy of suffering in their hearts. Nobody could be happy under such circumstances! The Bible says that *"the joy of the Lord"* is the strength of the Christian.

This brings us to the next big subject . . . that of suffering. It is said that because Jesus Christ was the Son of God, suffering to Him was all the more intense because He was more sensitive to pain in all its forms.

We often think of His physical suffering when we observe the Lord's Supper, but do we really understand? I believe that only those who know what suffering means can adequately glimpse a measure of His sufferings. It cannot be interpreted in any other way. Perhaps this is why Christians who suffer affliction become so much more mature than those who escape it?

To get back to His sufferings, we are told by Josephus that apart from the indignities heaped upon our Lord the night before His crucifixion, when He was spat upon, buffetted and His beard plucked from His cheeks, the scourge which followed was so cruelly intense that often the strongest of criminals died under its administration. The Roman authorities often called off this punishment before the victims died in order to see them writhe in the last moments of agony on the cross. A man's back was often pulverised by the intensity of this beating as the bits of bone and iron tore into the flesh. Yet He bore every lash for us. It was not called off when He stood before His persecutors. That is why the Scriptures declare, *"He hath no form nor comeliness . . . "* In His radiant manhood He was a sun-tanned young man who attracted young children to His knees. It was in the hour of His suffering that *"We hid as it were our faces from Him"*.

I well remember when I fell heavily into a bed of coral on a glorious coastal strip in the Fiji Islands. The razor-sharp rock neatly whipped out a huge piece of flesh from my limb like a surgeon's knife. They rushed me to the doctor on the back of a truck, only to discover that he was away for the weekend. His wife did the best she could with a large hessian needle, finding it difficult to pierce my tough skin with the crude instrument. That was bad enough, but whenever I put my leg to the ground, even for a few seconds, the pain was unbearable. They carried me from place to place to minister God's Word, and my thoughts turned to Christ on the cross. His acute sufferings were more understandable now.

A few years ago I fell heavily from a ten foot ladder just two hours before my daughter's wedding. As I lay in agony on the floor, a Baptist minister arrived on the scene and we shared together something of our Lord's sufferings, which he brought into his address the next day. Then the doctor turned up and wrongly diagnosed the case; instead of reducing what he thought was a dislocation, he wrenched out four broken pieces of bone and pushed the lot into the muscle bed, resulting in such pain that I was soon vomiting in distress. After two hours on the operating table I was told by the surgeon that I would experience much more pain. He was right! For weeks I was unable to sleep. I had a fresh conception of our Lord's sufferings on the cross. It became relevant, and I could understand more clearly.

On one occasion during the celebration of the Lord's Supper in our local church in Melbourne, we listened with rapt attention to a discourse on His sufferings by a godly evangelist who had visited many countries with his caravan. Suddenly he stopped and looked at us intently.

"Why, what's the matter with you all?" he asked. "I don't see any tears! When I speak to the folk in Russia about the sufferings of our Lord, there isn't a dry eye. You see, they know what suffering is, and can interpret it."

We were stunned to silence. What did we know in our affluence just what it was to suffer for Christ? Did we understand anything about it at all?

But our Lord's physical sufferings were nothing compared to the suffering He endured in His soul and spirit. Although racking bodily pain can be almost unendurable, it cannot be compared with the anguish produced by unfaithfulness, disloyalty, or a betrayal of trust. The unspeakable injury imposed by delinquents on their godly parents, or the cruelty inflicted upon a sweet Christian woman by a profligate husband, or the dreadful loss of security endured by children because of separated parents—these tragedies of life produce a far more intense suffering than anything physical! A broken engagement; a business failure; a nervous breakdown; a criminal assault; drug and dope addiction; an unwanted child; all these and much more produce intense suffering in the soul and spirit which nothing, apart from the grace of God, can alleviate.

I believe this is the crux of the matter concerning our Lord's crucifixion. Quite apart from the physical agony. He suffered in His spirit as no man has ever suffered, to bring us to God. You see, *"He who knew no sin, was made sin for us, that we might become the righteousness of God in Him."* For someone who hated sin, to be made what He loathed, despised, and hated, is indeed suffering!

How can this ever be adequately explained? How can the human mind grasp it's significance? *"Oh make me understand it, help me to take it in, what it meant to thee, the Holy One, to bear away my sin."*

Some years ago I experienced something which I will never forget, and I am sure I can never be the same again. For the first time in my life I really hated sin. I have often preached against sin. I have ministered God's answer to sin. I have spent many hours showing from God's Word how Christ can give us victory over sin. I have regarded sin as something to be shunned, to be guarded against, or to be repudiated in the Christian life, but on this occasion something happened to make me really hate sin.

A beautiful young girl of about sixteen years of age, wrote asking how she could get back to God. She had been a radiant witness for Christ at High School where her testimony had simply glowed for the Lord.

Upon leaving school, she discovered that there would be a waiting period of some months before she could train as a nurse. She had accordingly applied for a temporary job as a waitress, and I blame her Christian

113

parents for ever allowing her to answer an advertisement which took her a hundred miles from home into a strange environment. She later admitted that deep down inside she knew she should never have applied for the position. Anyway this lovely young girl was soon utterly ruined by an immoral crowd who took delight in dragging her down into their debauched way of living. Her parents detected in her letters that something was wrong, but never dreamed what had actually happened.

After some months she sickened of it all, and sought to get right with God . . . but however hard she tried, however much she confessed her sin to the Lord, there was no answer. She was unable to find the peace she once knew, and to enter again into the joy of salvation. Hence the letter. Could I help her to get back to God? I answered to the best of my ability and heard no more from her.

Some time later I was conducting evangelistic meetings in one of Australia's modern cities and experiencing much blessing. The church was packed to capacity. Many had come out for Christ that evening. I remember it well because one of the oldest men I have ever met found the Lord that night.

During the counselling which followed I was informed that a young woman insisted on seeing me personally in the enquiry room.

When everyone else had left I found myself sitting opposite one of the most beautiful young teenagers I have ever seen. Her face was stained with tears, and she implored me to help her. "Mr. Stokes, I just can't get back to God. Please help me . . . "

It was the young girl who had previously written to me. As I looked across the table and saw what sin had done in the life of this lovely creature, something inside me seemed to snap, and I hated sin as never before. I saw something of its dreadful diabolical nature. It was as though a cruel hand had crushed a

114

fragrant blossom, and now it was wilting on the scrap heap of life. My spirit was indignant, outraged, and righteously angry with sin. But I also saw something else. I saw the Lord, who hated sin far more than I did, being made sin for this despairing girl that she might be cleansed from its dreadful guilt and power. I entered into a new experience of what it must have cost Him to die on the cross, bearing the very weight of every single sin in order to redeem mankind from its clutches. I imagined this girl to be my own daughter, and I wept at the thought of it. She wept with me. It was indeed a sacred moment, but how was she to get back to the Saviour? How could she be restored, cleansed and forgiven into a new experience with God? The way of a transgressor is hard, and she still had to face up to further awful implications of her sin. Confession to the Lord alone was not enough. She had tried this without success. What was the next step?

My reply was no easy way out. I explained that as a young teenager, responsible to her Christian parents, she would have to share the situation with them. Her sin had also made her a deceiver. They had no idea what was involved. They imagined her to be the pure and lovely girl she had been, and every time she sat with them at the table she was putting on a pretence. I could see no other course but that of telling them what I knew.

At this she cried out in anguish . . . "It would kill them if they knew," and sobbed uncontrollably.

"No, it won't," I replied. "But in any case, why didn't you think of that before?"

We left after a time of prayer together during which we committed the whole situation to the Lord. A few days later I received another letter, telling of the consequences.

"When I got home," she wrote, "I determined to have it out with Mum and Dad, and waiting until my younger brothers and sisters had gone to bed, I shared everything with them. We all wept. But, Mr. Stokes, you were right . . . I've got back to God! I hate my sin, myself, and all the involvements of the past few months. I wish I had never gone to that place. I wish I could forget the whole horrible nightmare, but the Lord has cleansed and forgiven me. I've got back to God."

It was for the joy that was set before the Lord that He endured the cross . . . the joy of bringing a new creation into being through the birth pangs of Calvary; the joy of knowing that millions would be redeemed and set free from the law of sin and death; the joy of restoring and regenerating hell-deserving sinners from death and destruction . . . yes, the joy of bringing you and me back to God from the dark paths of sin. Christ's sufferings were made all the more intense by your sin and mine. He hated sin, and still does, yet He was made sin, that you and I might be made the righteousness of God in Him.

We are living in days of sub-normal standards, when sin is no longer regarded as such by the majority of those around us. If we can listen to our TV programmes and get thoroughly accustomed to bad language and disgusting presentations without feeling nauseated, we are not likely to understand the sufferings of our Lord. If we can accept situations of compromise which seek to crucify Him afresh, without registering any form of protest within, then we are in grave danger of losing our spiritual ground to the Enemy. But more than that. We will have lost our joy already . . . the joy of a life surrendered to the will of God; and when our joy goes, then everything else goes with it. Remember, the *"joy of the Lord is our strength"* and this inevitably comes through suffering.

Yes, *"It was for the joy that was set before Him that He endured the cross and despising the shame, and is set down at the right hand of God."* Have you ever thanked Him for this? Why not do so now?

21   Festival of Light

Blessed are the pure in heart.
(Matt. 5: 8)

Many years ago, three warriors of the Christian faith were burned at the stake on the roadway outside Balliol College, in Oxford. One of them was heard to say, "We shall this day light such a candle by God's grace in England as I trust shall never be put out."

Today this light is dim. Our country, once famed for its integrity, is now renowned for its immorality. The aftermath of two world wars, coupled with a subsequent breakdown in marriage ties, has resulted in a gradual disappearance of spiritual standards. Material prosperity has succeeded in creating a row of tarnishable chromium-plated false gods, and their deluded worshippers bow in adoration only to find no real satisfaction in life.

The present generation revolted, and throwing overboard all restraint has sought to express itself in lives of total inhibition. Supported by the mass media of the press, radio and TV, and backed by the vested interests of pornography, every encouragement has been given to exploit the situation. Many of our laws are totally inadequate to stem the tide of evil which is slowly but surely engulfing our beloved land.

We all know the sad consequences. Sexual perversion and criminal assault is on the increase; drug addiction is a major problem to our society; the breakdown in home life is almost universal; to say nothing of the alarming increase in venereal disease amongst young children; and abortions abound. The church, in

117

the main, has remained strangely silent.

I address my remarks to all in our midst who claim to give allegiance to the Christian faith. The state of our nation can largely be blamed on those who claim to know the Light, but who have never revealed it to others. We need to repent and put our house in order before we can expect others to do the same.

The Festival of Light was launched by a joining together of multitudes of people all over the United Kingdom in a peaceful kind of demonstration against the increasing trend towards moral pollution and pornography. Many hundreds of beacons were kindled simultaneously in different parts of the country, to alert Britain to the danger of an invasion. This was an old time method, warning the nation of an impending enemy. Today that enemy is a traitor within our midst, a powerful invader which threatens the moral fibre of our once great nation. The sea of moral pollution and the tide of pornographic evil is sloshing around our very doors, threatening our very existence.

But the beacon is not only a warning. It is a light which symbolises a new call to love, purity and family life. The great National Festival of Light culminated in a huge rally in Trafalgar Square followed by a pop concert in Hyde Park to reflect the Christian angle. We demonstrated that "moral pollution needs a solution". We declared that there IS an answer to the problem, not by a self righteous denunciation, but by a Christian pronunciation! We believe that the great aspirations and hope of love on which our own civilisation was founded can be rediscovered in a personal relationship with God, through Jesus Christ, our Lord. We know that all that is good and beautiful in literature and art can be regained in this way.

We as Christians must declare and demonstrate God's standards in the moral realm of sex relationships. These are unchangeable and there are no exceptions, but I think we must rid ourselves of the image of

118

Victorian morality. Prudery is not found in the Christian faith. Putting petticoats on the legs of the dining table is no solution to the problem. The human body is sacred and beautiful when dedicated to the purposes of God. We Christians do not hide our heads in the sand. We do not run away from nudity as such. It is because Christ dwells in our hearts by faith, and we see from His standpoint the wonder of God's creative and redemptive purposes, that we can thank Him every day for the way in which we are made. The old human nature which was ours from birth has become subservient to a new spiritual power which we received when we were born of God. To us sex is nothing to be ashamed of, but something wonderful and beautiful with which to glorify God in the most sacred of all human relationships.

The Christian standards of morality can be summed up as follows . . . ABSOLUTE ABSTINENCE OUTSIDE MARRIAGE AND ABSOLUTE FAITHFULNESS WITHIN. That is the simple Gospel declaration of love, hope and joy within the sanctity of a home life dedicated to God.

Starting with Christian love affairs, there is to be no physical sexual indulgence outside the sacred bonds of marriage. The condition of membership within the early church makes this perfectly plain. Fornication or sexual relationships between unmarried people are strictly forbidden. Of course, this does not mean that those who had fallen in this way were to be excluded from the fellowship of the church. If they had truly repented and stood against this form of social evil, and had repudiated it as forgiven sinners, they were welcome. I am merely stating the declared Christian standards for young and old. I would sooner proclaim that Christ is a fence at the top of a cliff preventing folk from falling over the edge, than to declare Him as an ambulance down below waiting to pick up the victims. Of course He is both. I am sure you know what I mean. May I suggest that all those reading this make a solemn declaration before God that with His help they will seek to maintain the Christian standards of sexual morality in their own circles, and demonstrate His standards before others. There is no need for me to refer to all forms of sexual perversion, forbidden and condemned in the Scriptures; they invoke God's judgement individually, socially, and nationally.

Faithfulness within marriage is an absolute Christian virtue. There is a great breakdown here. We Christians must bear witness to the Light in this direction. The sanctity of a Christian home is the only guarantee that the rising generation will sit up and take notice. It is Christ Himself who makes the home such a wonderful place. We Christians must increasingly open our homes to those around us that they may see this reality for themselves and share in the wonder of it all. A Christian home provides the backbone of a great nation, and is often the spiritual birthplace of noble men and women.

Now a word on pornography. This is not difficult for the Christian to define. Any attempt by way of literature, films, or supposed art, to defile the mind by destroying the sacredness of sex in any wise, is pornographic. Cheap paperback erotic novels, crude illustrations or photographs of the sex act, or perversions of such, can all be classed under this heading. We Christians must take a stand against all forms of pornography for our children's sake. There is already a threatened invasion of our schools.

We light a beacon of warning. We also invite those whose lives have been soiled and spoiled by moral sin to come to Christ for His wonderful cleansing and forgiveness. THE LIGHT OF THE WORLD DOES NOT CONDEMN. HE KNOWS THAT ALL OF US ARE SINNERS BY NATURE. HE INVITES US TO COME TO HIM PERSONALLY TO EXPERIENCE THE FRAGRANT CLEANSING OF A COMPLETELY NEW LIFE, AS HE FORGIVES AND FORGETS THE OLD. The deepest-dyed sinner can find perfect peace, cleansing and freedom through simple faith in Him. The fact is that we can exchange our old sordid lives for new spiritual clean ones. This is the glorious truth of Christian conversion.

May the beacon which the Festival lit in many places spell the doom of a threatened invasion which is much more serious than the Battle of Britain. This time it is the Battle for Britain! We will certainly be criticised and jeered at by many, but this is to be expected. I appeal to those of you who stand with me to *"put on the armour of light"* and in so doing to *"cast off the works of darkness"*. Who knows, but at this late hour, our country may be spared the inevitable consequences of God's wrath and judgment as we vigorously declare His salvation to the sons of men.

The beacon was lit in joyous anticipation of a new era of hope and faith in Christian principles, as a declaration of our faithfulness to the highest and best in Christ's Name. This was backed up by the proclamations made in Trafalgar Square for presentation to the Government, the Church, and the mass media. May God give us the courage of our convictions to stand up consistently for truth, purity, and love, which could pave the way for a mighty spiritual revival in bringing many out of darkness and slavery into His most marvellous light and liberty.

NOTE   The author fully realises that there are other moral problems besides the sex problem, which all contribute towards the present decline. However, it is generally agreed that the sudden gigantic escalation of immorality on this level is the chief cause for alarm, and that is why he has emphasised this particular aspect in his message first delivered at the Festival of Light, in Cirencester, and later over the "Gems of Grace" radio programme from Monte Carlo and Bonaire.

22   Bonaire Tragedy

*Thanks be to God who giveth us the
victory.*   (1 Cor. 15: 57)

It was a glorious day in the sunny Caribbean. I had
just arrived on my first visit to Bonaire, a small island
only fifteen minutes' flight from Curaçao, the famous
oiling port in the Netherlands Antilles. The weather
was hot and I decided to explore the coral beds only
a stone's throw from where I was staying with the
young station manager of Trans World Radio's powerful transmitters. Wearing a pair of underwater glasses
I was soon diving for shells and swimming alongside the
most beautiful tropical fish imaginable. This was no
new pastime, for I had spent many hours in the South
Sea Islands in Fiji and Samoa exploring the fairyland
of breathtaking colour, taking care not to tread on
any suspicious looking stone or rock which might prove
to be fatal. We always wore rubber shoes when on
the reef for this very purpose, as many deadly fish
disguised and camouflaged in their beautiful surroundings are ready to inject their venomous poison into
any trespasser. I remember hauling a deadly stone-fish
on board in the Cook Straits off the coast of Northern
Queensland's Great Barrier Reef, to the consternation
of my friend who was a local banana planter. On
another occasion, in Samoa, I jumped out of my canoe
almost on top of an enormous red starfish which
attracted my attention. It was a sight to behold, but
protruding from each of it's "stars" was a long sharp
needle full of venomous poison. My Samoan friend
told me that the only remedy for removing the deadly

122

stuff was to get hold of the starfish quickly and carefully and place its soft underpart over the wound when it would gradually suck its own poison out of the system. Food for thought! That which took a matter of seconds to inject, took hours to remove. How much like sin is this poison! As I swam amongst my new companions enjoying the refreshing coolness of these clear waters of the blue Caribbean, I was totally unaware of a tragedy that was taking place only a few miles away close to the great TWR transmitter, and in those very waters.

I was slowly making my way up to the house on the edge of the beach, when I saw the young manager's wife talking on the phone in a very agitated way. As I approached, she said, "One of our missionaries who has been out skin-diving is missing. We had better go along with the others to see if anything can be done to locate him." We drove to the spot to find a number of TWR missionaries standing helplessly by, while a launch was carrying out investigations. It was then we learned the tragic facts of the case.

Our missionaries in Bonaire work long hours, and one of their favourite pastimes is skin-diving—that is, donning compressed air equipment and swimming under the reef to explore the beauties as I had done, only in much deeper water. Three of them, including a father and son, had been together when something went wrong with one of the compressed air tanks. This man was unaccustomed to diving, although he had spent long hours studying its technique and had remarked to his wife only a few hours before he had left the house that it could be quite a risky business. He had apparently surfaced to make adjustments, but when joining the others something serious must have happened. He panicked and then seized hold of one of the other's oxygen mask, tearing it completely from him. The victim surfaced immediately, but was almost drowned in the attempt as he swallowed much water on the way up. In the meantime the other young man, who had seen his father surface, in complete disregard for his own safety, offered his mask to the struggling man below. He just had time to see him decline the offer, when he decided to surface immediately to go in search of his father whom he found in an exhausted condition coughing up blood. Dragging him to safety he did the only wise thing . . . tore along to the TWR studios and incoherently tried to explain the situation to the rest.

In next to no time rescuers were on the way, but it was too late. There was no sign of the poor man and a boat was launched to search for him. It was at this stage we joined the rest. I shall never forget the agonised look on the faces of those missionaries as they realised the serious nature of the situation. It was too late to hope for anything now, and the thoughts of everyone were with his wife and family who were totally ignorant of this disaster. A short time elapsed before his body was found and brought to shore. It was a sad time indeed.

Most of the missionaries were young marrieds, who had no experience of sharing such situations with each other and they felt completely helpless. It was hard enough to have to break the news, quite apart from offering comfort. What can one do at such times? I was an older man who had been through some deep waters myself. Maybe I could help?

The next morning I learned that the young wife would see nobody, and it was most unlikely that she would see me. I had never met her before. Committing the whole situation to the Lord, I ventured to offer some comfort and was soon knocking on her door. It was answered by one of her friends who repeated that she would see nobody. "I think she will see me," I said. "May I please come in?" The request was granted and I soon found myself tapping on the door of the room into which she had locked herself, asking for a brief interview.

After a few moments the door opened and I was alone with the distraught young wife, who immediately broke down with great sobs and tears. This was exactly what the doctor had ordered, and it was a great relief as there had been no emotional outburst up to that moment. I said nothing for some considerable time as all the pent up emotion exploded in this way and then we talked quietly.

"Jean," I said . . . "there are only two solutions to your immediate problem. You can either clench your fist in God's face or place your hands into Christ's nail-pierced ones and claim His wonderful grace to go through this with Him. I know of no other choice. What do you decide to do? After a while she slowly and deliberately, said, "I'll put my hands into His and keep them there!" We had a wonderful time of prayer and Jean rose from her knees with such a radiant look in her face that we knew the victory was already hers in His Name. How we rejoiced together in this!

Jean's testimony was fantastic. At the funeral service, when I was requested to speak, she sat in the front with her three little children as a wonderful witness to the Lord's saving grace in her life. Hundreds gathered for that service and it was a further opportunity of preaching the Gospel to many who had never heard it before. Jean's testimony was an unforgettable confirmation of this, and even the Governor of the island who attended the funeral was greatly impressed. As we laid the body to rest in a small graveyard nearby, Jean was a tower of strength to those who had felt so inadequate to share their grief and sorrow with her. She flatly refused to have the body flown to his native home town in the States and said that his testimony would continue just where the Lord had taken him Home. It was a brave decision, by a brave little woman who had received from the Lord Himself the strength to overcome her sad and difficult circumstances.

To those young missionaries it was nothing short of a miracle that the Lord should have brought me to Bonaire just a few hours before this tragedy took place. They said there was nobody amongst them who had the maturity of experience to deal with just such a situation as this and they saw the Lord's Hand in it all. Jean's testimony was an inspiration and she continued to work in the office in Bonaire with a zeal for the Lord that surprised everybody. A few years ago Jean met a young Christian missionary who joined the staff for a short term and he was so taken with her radiant testimony that they are now happily married and working with the Missionary Aviation Fellowship in another part of the world. The children love their new "Daddy" and the story has a very happy ending. I was glad to have been of some assistance.

Whenever I swim in coral seas and dive for shells, or watch closely the movements of those brilliantly coloured tropical fish, I have something else to think about now . . . Jean's haunting moments of agony which have now given place to such times of rich blessing. Her first husband was a good man who did his job diligently for TWR before he was taken to be with his Lord. We shall never understand "why" this happened. All we know is that God's grace did something for Jean, something perhaps which might otherwise never have happened to her inner life, something she was able to share with others in the midst of her deepest sorrow and agony . . . something which has brought to pass the saying *"death shall be swallowed up in victory"*, at least in her experience. What about yours, my friend? How have you reacted to your circumstances? Has it been the clenched fist or the submitted hand?

Miracles take place when we cease to resist the Spirit of God and start to submit to Him instead. It is the easiest thing in the world for anyone of us to resist God steadfastly in the face of terrifying circumstances. Deep down inside is the haunting question, often unexpressed but it's there . . . "Why should it happen to me?" Jean went through all that because she was only human. It was when she calmly refused to allow herself to be governed by the circumstances and submitted to the claims of her Lord and Saviour, that she was able to live above them for the first time. It was then she became such a tower of strength to those who felt their own inadequacy in bringing her the comfort she needed. It always works that way. Oh, my friend, if your heartbreaking circumstances have got you beat, how about handing over the reins to the Lord Jesus Christ Who alone has the capacity and the authority to deal with every situation so that you can rise above them and not be defeated any more? *"Thanks be to God who giveth us the victory through our Lord Jesus Christ."*